What people are saying about

Flowering Into Awareness

This book truly is a manifesto for our modern age in which
Pathik Strand explores our real nature, consciousness, that
which is beyond time and space. He demonstrates in detail
how the current materialistic paradigm – that we are all
separate entities living in a world that exists independently
of consciousness – is the basis of our individual and collective
suffering and the insanity of our world. Pathik shows that it
is only by coming to self-knowledge of our real nature that
transformation is possible and a new world can emerge. This
is not a path of spiritual effort and discipline to achieve a goal,
we are this awareness right now, nothing needs to be added,
only to allow this spontaneous understanding to blossom. The
understanding that we are universal consciousness is explored
in depth and breadth; this truth emanates from every page of an
inspiring book.
Billy Doyle, Author of *Yoga in the Kashmir Tradition: the art of
listening. Following the teachings of Jean Klein* and *The Mirage of
Separation*

Also by this Author

All This is That
ISBN: 978-0-95656-400-9

Flowering Into Awareness

A Spiritual Manifesto for the 21st Century

Flowering Into Awareness

A Spiritual Manifesto for the 21st Century

Pathik Strand

BOOKS

Winchester, UK
Washington, USA

JOHN HUNT PUBLISHING

First published by O-Books, 2021
O-Books is an imprint of John Hunt Publishing Ltd., 3 East St., Alresford,
Hampshire SO24 9EE, UK
office@jhpbooks.com
www.johnhuntpublishing.com
www.o-books.com

For distributor details and how to order please visit the 'Ordering' section on our website.

ISBN: 978 1 78904 751 6
978 1 78904 752 3 (ebook)
Library of Congress Control Number: 2020923777

A CIP catalogue record for this book is available from the British Library.

Design: Stuart Davies

UK: Printed and bound by CPI Group (UK) Ltd, Croydon, CR0 4YY
Printed in North America by CPI GPS partners

We operate a distinctive and ethical publishing philosophy in
all areas of our business, from our global network of authors to
production and worldwide distribution.

Contents

Dedicated to
The Great Spirit
That shines as
"I AM"
Within your Heart

A Poem at Dawn

Silently poised on the brink of annihilation
We witness the emergence of that which never dies
From dizzying heights, a distant call descends
Emerging out of dim shadows with a soft whisper
Like a song slowly unfolding from within a dream
Clearly audible though still veiled and hazy
Crying out with love and mercy at the break of dawn
It is relentless and unforgiving, yet loving and gentle
Across aeons of forgotten time and space
As we meet again and again and again
Rejoicing in the ancient game of joining and parting
A soothing truth tenderly emerges:
Only that day dawns to which we are awake

… and the truth will set you free

It comes as a surprise to me that I am starting this book by quoting a passage from the Bible, because I'm neither a Christian nor religious in any conventional sense of the word. However, I am happy to acknowledge that there are many words of wisdom in the Bible, as well as in the scriptures of other religions. Even though I don't tend to spend a lot of time poring over ancient religious texts, I'm always delighted when a gold nugget like this one comes my way. As far as I've been able to ascertain, the full quotation is, "You shall know the truth, and the truth will set you free," and it can be found in the Gospel According to John, 8:32. There is a great deal of wisdom in this statement, because spiritual realisation is very much centred around authentic insight and embodiment of the truth, as opposed to having just some kind of mere intellectual understanding of it.

In this first chapter I will try to give you a general idea of what this book is about, what I think is the root cause of mankind's many problems, and also the way out of our misery into a world of harmony and peace. To me it is evident that a deep and experiential knowledge of who we are as well as the consistent and passionate manifestation of unconditional love in our lives are of the utmost importance for our deeply troubled world to change from chaos, pain, misery and conflict into a world overflowing with creativity, love and happiness. Yes, I am absolutely convinced that this is possible, and as we go along I will try to explain to you why that is so and what it will take.

To give you a feeling of where I'm coming from, maybe we could try a little experiment using your imagination. Imagine that you are living in a world where there is no war, conflict, violence, hate, dishonesty, fear, greed, exploitation, poverty, pollution or any of all the other horrors that our world is

1

presently so full of. Imagine that your home planet is one of harmony, joy, love, peace, freedom and boundless creativity. Everybody is kind, helpful and cooperative, and nature is treated with love, respect and sensitivity, instead of being exploited, raped and destroyed. Imagine what a joyous, beautiful and fulfilling life this would be for everybody. Now imagine that for whatever reason you have to go and live on planet Earth during the first few decades of the 21st century, directly and personally experiencing all the misery, problems and pain of our world. Wouldn't you feel as if you had entered a madhouse, a world that is so completely and utterly insane that you wouldn't have thought that it was possible if you hadn't experienced it for yourself?

A severely dysfunctional world of unbelievable complexity, endless conflicts, environmental destruction and exceptional misery is unfortunately precisely the kind of world we have created and are presently living in, yet we have become so accustomed to it that we hardly ever think of the world as mad. It is as if most of us have become blind to the insanity that is now so prevalent, so completely ubiquitous in all areas of life, that we consider it all perfectly normal. Well, it is actually normal in the sense that our collective madness is so common that it is the norm, but that hardly makes it sane. We seem to have accepted this kind of lunatic world as something inevitable, even natural, but it is of course neither inevitable nor natural.

Whenever abject and despicable human behaviour like hate, greed, jealousy, exploitation, dishonesty and so on rears its ugly head, we tend to think of it as human nature, but nothing could be further from the truth. Human nature is most definitely not one of greed, hate, fear and all the rest of it. If anything, what is natural for humans is to manifest love, peace, cooperation, kindness, harmony and honesty. These are all qualities that are given to us quite abundantly by life itself, in fact they are natural expressions of what we truly are. However, for the most part we seem to do our best to cover them up as much as we possibly can, opting instead for selfishness, possessiveness, insensitivity, greed and fear.

It doesn't have to be like this. There is another way, a way in which we can all live peacefully and harmoniously, in abundant creativity, with great love for all life. All our neurotic and dysfunctional behaviour is possible only because we insist on remaining ignorant of our true nature, of who we are. It is self-knowledge in the most fundamental sense that is lacking in our world. That is the root cause of all our woes and problems. Everything else flows from this basic core of ignorance of who we are in essence.

For most of known human history, the majority of people have been completely convinced that they are an ego, a separate entity, and that we all have to fight and struggle endlessly for our survival and prosperity. This conviction has been so powerful that most people have never even thought to question whether this is the case or not. It is this fundamental misunderstanding that gives rise to selfishness, which in turn produces greed, fear and all the rest of it. As long as we define ourselves as a separate entity, an ego, belonging to a particular race, religion, nation, family, political or social group and so on, or we think of who we are in terms of career, accomplishments, personal talents or suchlike, the madness will continue in one form or another.

What we fundamentally are has nothing to do with any of the above. Our true nature is that of pure, luminous, limitless, impersonal, universal consciousness. There is only ever one consciousness, and it is in fact exactly the so-called ordinary consciousness that is aware of these words and their meaning. The full knowledge, understanding and embodiment of this simple fact won't give you worldly riches, superhuman powers, great charisma or a halo round your head, but it does have the potential to change your life in ways that you might not have expected. I should also add that this kind of understanding isn't really a personal achievement, something you can get for yourself, but more on that later. Once a majority of humanity arrives at this understanding and lets go of the old, false identification with ego and limited self, life on Earth will start to be transformed for the better in ways we cannot even begin to imagine.

However, it is important to understand that what we call the ego isn't necessarily and inherently bad or evil. It becomes a problem only to the degree that it is taken as one's primary identity. The ego is only a makeshift identity, and there is actually no core unique ego or person inside you somewhere that is always fixed. The ego is in a state of continuous flux, and even in the seemingly most selfish of us, it isn't always there. At the very least, in deep dreamless sleep, there is no ego, in fact there is no experience or world at all in the way we usually think of it, only the profound peace and silence of the being that you truly are. When I use the word ego in this book, it is only to make it easier to refer to that process within us that in various forms manifests as greed, fear, selfishness and so on. The ego itself is neither good nor bad, because it's just a temporary fluctuation of thoughts, memories, feelings, habits and conditioning. It should naturally and effortlessly cease to exist whenever it's not needed, but because virtually everybody takes it as their personal identity, it seems to be there almost all the time. We all make use of this kind of fictional ego entity, and even the most highly revered spiritual masters engage with the process of ego, but that's not a problem as long as it's not taken as one's true identity.

A different aspect of mistaking one's true identity to be a separate ego-self located somewhere inside your head so to speak is the unquestioned assumption that what we usually think of as the material world or the physical universe is the true, fundamental reality, and that it exists independently of consciousness. It automatically follows on from this belief that mind and consciousness are nothing but by-products of some inexplicable process in the human brain.

Many philosophers and religious pundits have argued against the philosophy of materialism, and you may well be familiar with the ancient Indian concept of Maya, which essentially says that the world of the senses is illusory. That is of course the polar opposite of maintaining that the world as we see it is ultimately real. However, it is much closer to the truth to see the world as real, but only in the sense of being a manifestation or modulation of universal consciousness. In other words, what we think of as physical reality is not the source of consciousness and neither is the world we live in an illusion. Quite the contrary, the world of the senses is certainly real, but only by virtue of ultimately being an expression of consciousness itself.

Seeing the so-called material world as existing independently of consciousness, and seeing oneself as a separate entity in this world are but two sides of the same coin. This kind of materialist self-centredness will inevitably bring about self-deception, illusion, ignorance, separation and conflict, and is the root cause of all the world's problems and whatever challenges humanity may be facing.

This book is written as an attempt to help you answer the question of who you are in a direct and authentic way, and also to make you understand how the realisation of your true nature is the key to the transformation of human consciousness and the emergence of a new world of peace and harmony. The full flowering of humanity's potential, in fact our ultimate destiny, depends precisely on the dawning of this realisation on human consciousness.

I should also mention that when I use an expression like human consciousness, it really just means our uniquely human expression of universal consciousness, and it would perhaps be better to use expressions like human mind or human psyche.

What's important to bear in mind is that consciousness itself is indivisible and all-inclusive, and totally beyond anything that can be described or defined. All definitions and descriptions can only impose limitations on that which is truly limitless and beyond all forms, so human consciousness is therefore only just another flavour or manifestation of that which is the source and essence of all.

The fact that you have picked up this book, and may even have decided to read it, more than likely means that you are ready for realising who you are if you haven't already done so. You may indeed have been feeling, as I often have, that you really have landed on the wrong planet, that you just don't seem to fit in, often feel like a lone voice in the wilderness, and that you are struggling to come to terms with seemingly being very different from almost everybody else. This is actually a very good point of departure, and should be cause for celebration, not for despair. The path from this realisation to knowing who you are is not very long, because it is very fertile ground for grasping the truth that what you essentially are is nothing but universal consciousness itself, the one consciousness in which all phenomena seem to arise, exist and disappear.

What I have outlined in these few introductory paragraphs is the most essential insight and the main theme of this book. If you have the patience and necessary interest, you should be able to grasp the truth of who you are for yourself, and eventually embody the reality of it in your life. Certain ideas are likely to be repeated in different ways throughout the book, but that's only to make it more likely that they will be seriously considered and understood. Some of what's presented here may be unfamiliar to you, and if that's the case, I would encourage you to take some time to let it sink in, without automatically accepting or discarding what you are reading. Try it on for size so to speak and see if you can make it real in your own experience. Nobody knows what this journey has in store for

you, but the full realisation of your true nature, in whatever
way that might come about, has the potential to change your life
and the world forever.

Your true nature

The words spiritual and spirituality are in fairly heavy use these days, yet it's not always entirely clear what people mean when they use them. These words can refer to almost anything on a scale ranging from fairly fundamentalist, orthodox and traditional forms of religious practice and theology, right through to a variety of highly unconventional and speculative New Age beliefs and practices. Because there are so many different interpretations of the words spiritual and spirituality, I should therefore explain what I refer to when using them.

The way I see it, spirituality and a spiritual way of life must necessarily include the qualities of compassion and unconditional love, mindfulness and presence, and a high degree of authentic self-knowledge. It can be argued that self-knowledge is the most important of these, because unconditional love and being present in the eternity of now are the spontaneous and natural flavours of true self-knowledge. The realisation of your true nature also means that you also know that form and formless are one, and that everything that seems to exist on the level of form is merely an expression of that which is beyond and independent of all forms.

Because I see self-knowledge as being more important than anything else, I am also of the opinion that the most fundamental question you can ever ask yourself is the one that goes straight to the core of your own identity at its most basic level. This question is usually verbalised either as, "Who am I?" or "What am I?" I tend to think that the latter is the more potent way of asking it because the word "who" seems somehow to indicate a clearly defined somebody, whereas asking, "What am I?" is more open-ended. However, this is just a matter of personal preference, and one cannot be said to be objectively superior to the other.

8

Throughout the ages, countless people have asked themselves questions like: "Who am I?" and "What is the nature of my true being?" Many of us will have tried to find out who or what we really are at some point during our lives, perhaps particularly while still fairly young, but only a relatively small minority of us have enough patience and passion to ever get to the heart of this quest. People all over the world have for the most part come to seek answers to this inquiry in terms of whatever role they happen to be playing in life. The only problem with this approach is that one's true identity is not something that can be defined on the basis of culture, upbringing, religious beliefs, social or political conditions, family, or any other conditional circumstances. The truth of who you are goes much deeper and is much more profound than anything to do with your personal life and circumstances. Regardless of who you think you might be, you are certainly not that little ego person that you have always been told that you are and that you came to believe in at quite a young age. What you are, what we all are, is in fact something so obvious, simple and straightforward that most people tend to overlook it completely.

For the vast majority of people, it is common to think of one's identity in terms of one's past. After all, we seem to be born in a particular place at a particular time, into a certain family, and into specific cultural, religious, social and political circumstances. For most of us these things tend to become the key factors in determining for ourselves who we are, and we often use them to define our most fundamental sense of identity. You might think and feel that who you are is a result of everything that has ever happened to you, and in terms of your personality that might very well be the case.

However, your personality is not your true identity, but more like a role you are playing, or a mask that you are wearing. What has happened throughout your life is not of that much relevance when it comes to realising who you are, because regardless of what happens to you, none of it can touch the fundamental reality of what you are. In the context of realising your true nature, the whole history of your life is of no more substance or importance than a quickly forgotten dream, and it's got only whatever meaning you assign to it. The reason for this is that whatever has happened in your life can never touch or change what you are at the deepest core of your being.

Life is not what we think it is, and we are not what we think we are. We have all been victims of a kind of automatic process of conditioning right from the day we were born, and this conditioning is so powerful and has been so successful, that it is very rare indeed for anyone to seriously question the fundamental worldview that is at the heart of this conditioning. The vast majority of us seem to be hapless victims of the kind of collective hypnosis that usually passes for upbringing and education. All the things our parents, teachers, priests and a host of other so-called experts have told us, and virtually hammered into us, have made most of us slowly but surely live our lives totally entangled in a veil of illusions, make-believe and prefabricated conclusions. This pattern is constantly being strengthened and kept alive by virtually everyone we meet and indeed by the whole structure of society. You could say that in a way we are on constant autopilot, and the sooner you realise this for yourself, the better.

We all exist within an intricately spun web of fundamentalist, shared beliefs, assumptions and conclusions. Most people seem to believe in certain things so wholeheartedly that they are automatically taken for granted. The most widespread belief in our culture, indeed the bedrock of most people's worldview, is that we are all separate entities existing in an objectively real external world made from matter, and that this world exists independently of consciousness. Virtually everybody is so convinced of this that it is hardly ever questioned by anyone. After all, it seems so obvious that this is how it is, and regardless of what kind of beliefs we might otherwise subscribe to, the certainty that we are separate beings existing in a material world that is external to and independent of consciousness is hardly ever shaken. This belief is shared by atheists and religious people alike, by people from all walks of life, irrespective of educational and vocational accomplishments, and whatever their social and cultural background might happen to be. Even within most of what can be described as contemporary spirituality this belief in duality and separation is the norm rather than the exception.

However, there are signs that this façade of dualistic deception is starting to develop some serious cracks, and it is indeed possible that this whole edifice of intricately structured illusion could soon come tumbling down. We are currently faced with the possibility of nothing short of a fundamental paradigm shift, and it is one that is essential for humanity to pass through if we are to evolve beyond selfishness and conflict, and thus fulfil our highest potential. The intellectual, materialistic and reductionist worldview that is currently predominant says that matter is primary and that everything else, including consciousness itself, developed from that. Within this paradigm, the so-called big bang created the universe as we know it, and by some unfathomable and unbelievably unlikely series of an almost infinite number of totally random events, life evolved on this insignificant little planet to the point where humans appeared with a brain sophisticated enough to create consciousness. This is a story of creation that is as fanciful and improbable as the Christian myth that God created the world in six days, all perfectly finished off and fully functional, and then being rather pleased with his almighty efforts allowed himself to put his feet up and take a breather on the seventh day.

The philosophy of materialism is often thought of as being scientifically proven, but materialism has nothing whatsoever to do with genuine science. While it is true that many scientists today subscribe to a materialistic worldview, that doesn't make the philosophy of materialism into scientifically proven fact. The truth of the matter is that it is nothing of the kind, but rather contemporary humanity's most cherished belief system, its most commonly accepted version of irrefutable truth. Most people don't seem to question any of the given tenets of materialism at all, but instead automatically accept them as scientifically proven, in spite of the fact that it's all just nothing but pure speculation. Moreover, this belief system is so ingrained and entrenched in most of us that nothing short of a miracle will be able to dismantle it.

The archaic and outdated paradigm within which contemporary culture still exists may have served some kind of purpose back in the day, but isn't it high time that such a thoroughly dysfunctional belief system is discarded and chucked in the bin for good? To think that matter is primary and that the brain somehow creates consciousness is like putting the cart before the horse and expecting that you're going to get somewhere. No true understanding is possible until the church of materialism is seen for the travesty it is, and thereby dismantled and abandoned for good.

The first thing that needs to happen in order to create a new paradigm that serves humanity and life on Earth much better than the one presently in vogue, is to realise and fully understand that consciousness is primary and that everything else springs from consciousness. In other words, we need to recognise that universal consciousness is what we all are. It is essential to realise that consciousness is the true nature of our being, and that it cannot be reduced to a mere by-product of the brain or just another phenomenon of life. Consciousness is the reality that cannot be further reduced. It is all-inclusive, all-pervasive and almighty in the sense that it truly is all. Everything is included within it, although from the point of view of consciousness itself, which is the only fully realistic and authentic point of view, there is neither within nor without.

Consciousness is the one fundamental reality. It exists both within and beyond time and space. There might be many bodies, many minds, multiple universes and levels of reality, but there is only ever one consciousness, and it is eternal, infinite and totally beyond what we can describe, define or understand. There is only ever this one consciousness, seemingly expressing itself as an innumerable variety of forms. The consciousness that is aware of this being written is exactly the same consciousness that is aware of reading and understanding these words, irrespective of whether the conditioned mind is agreeing or disagreeing with them.

The idea that anything can exist outside of consciousness, or that there is a reality independent of consciousness, is actually quite absurd, but it is an idea that is thoroughly embedded within the human psyche, and for that reason it is very difficult for most people to let go of it. Most of what's going on in our culture, in fact our entire civilisation, is built on this idea that the world has a reality that is independent of consciousness. That is absurd and in fact totally illogical, but you can understand that only if you realise that consciousness is primary, and that the brain, the body, the world, the universe and whatever else you can possibly think of all appear and disappear within consciousness.

You can verify for yourself that consciousness is primary and that from which everything else springs forth, because that is indeed your own direct experience. Consciousness is the light that brings everything to life, everything appears within consciousness, and all forms on all possible levels are in fact nothing but ever new modulations of consciousness. Consciousness forever remains, and all this other stuff is nothing but fleeting flimsy fluff that comes and goes, of no more importance or significance than what we give to it.

Without a revolution right at the core of the human psyche, humanity will never be able to live in peace and harmony, truly prosper and fulfil its potential. This revolution depends on each and every one of us understanding and deeply realising that impersonal, eternal, infinite, ordinary consciousness is all, and that it is indeed what we truly are. Consciousness is primary, the ultimate reality; everything else follows from that. Without consciousness, no existence, universe, world or reality is or can ever be possible. The brain, the mind, the body, the world, the universe, and whatever else that appears on the level of form all arise within consciousness. Everything appears, exists and disappears in consciousness. Everything is consciousness expressed through the medium of externalised form.

If you take only one thing with you from reading this book, let it be this: Universal consciousness is all there ever is. It is the essence and entire reality of what you are and what the world is. This realisation has the potential to bring about the transformation necessary for humanity to live in peace and harmony and thus reach its full flowering. It holds the key to a revolution in the collective human mind; a revolution that has the potential to leave selfishness, conflict, greed and fear behind forever, to make humanity embrace authentic altruism, generosity and love. If this were to happen, it should be obvious that life on Earth would be transformed for the better beyond all expectations and beyond anything we could ever imagine. Peace on Earth would finally be a reality, and not a second too soon if I may say so.

The eternal quest

The search for meaning, fulfilment, truth, enlightenment or whatever else you might want to call it is as old as humanity itself. But before we go any further in our search, let's stop right now and ask ourselves: Why do we search for anything at all? What is presently missing in our own lives to make us undertake this kind of exploration? Could it be that our way of living and our sense of identity leave something to be desired?

The irony of it all is that as far as the truth of who you are is concerned you don't actually have to search for it or do anything at all to realise it, quite simply because you are already it. Please understand that I am not suggesting that you should stop searching for truth, meaning or whatever else you fancy, quite the contrary. Whatever you try to do to realise the truth about who you are is perfectly fine. As long as you think that you need to do something to know who you are and realise enlightenment, you might as well get on with it. There is a delightful paradox here in the sense that the search itself may be necessary or at least helpful for many of us. Putting all your energy and passion into this kind of inner search seems to help burn away the obstacles to realising what was there in full view right from the start. When the truth about life and who you are finally dawns on you though, it does so not because of your efforts, but in spite of them.

The fact is that no matter what you do, where you go or what you may practise, you will essentially remain what you eternally are, namely consciousness itself. This holds true under all circumstances and regardless of what you might happen to be busying yourself with. You may even feel like you're going forward or that you're really getting somewhere, that you are developing spiritually and rising in consciousness, but the fact remains that you are still the consciousness, awareness, being that you always and eternally are, regardless of what happens. This is of course also the case if you're having great spiritual experiences along the way or if you reach rare and blissful states of mind. Throughout all of this the consciousness that you are remains the backdrop and witness to it all, holding everything in its compassionate embrace. It is always present, always all-accepting and always completely non-judgemental.

If you are still a spiritual seeker, you might be thinking that you are getting closer to your real, innermost self, but you already are your real innermost self, so how can you be getting any closer to it? This whole process of seeking and searching for answers and great mind-blowing experiences, enlightenment and the like is nothing but the mind trying to make its own dreams and fantasies come true. You may feel that you are really getting somewhere, especially if you are having deep and mind-expanding experiences, but you are still marching on the same spot, doing nothing more than trying to catch the wind. You might be making grand and noble efforts, but none of it can ever lead you to your intended destination – to who you are – because you are already that. Universal consciousness is always only one indivisible reality, even though it may seem to disguise itself in the innumerable forms of what we usually think of as life or reality. Everything spontaneously arises and naturally dissolves within universal consciousness, and no experience, reality or truth is possible without it.

No matter how hard you try to nail down, label or claim the truth as your own personal property, you are fighting a losing battle. Consciousness can never be defined, classified, labelled, owned or taken possession of, quite simply because it isn't a thing or a defined something or other, like an object apart from you. It is the ultimate subject in which all objects come and go, and from which all forms are made. It is totally beyond all forms, yet all forms are contained within it and made in its imageless image. All you can ever think, feel, dream, perceive and sense are just modulations of consciousness, temporary forms that fluctuate briefly throughout the ephemeral world of time and space. Nothing can ever harm, hurt, falsify or destroy the ultimate reality, whether we refer to it as consciousness, awareness, spirit, the divine, God or anything else. It depends on nothing else because there is nothing else than that, yet all the posturing, drama, comedy, absurdity, conflict and hullaballoo of the world can have no validity, reality or existence apart from consciousness. All this is that, and that's all there is to it.

All methods and techniques, no matter how sophisticated and advanced they are, have an almost imperceptible way of creating their own particular patterns that have a subtle way of imprisoning you. However, practising methods and techniques is perfectly all right, because as long as you think or feel that you haven't arrived, you will most effectively be able to burn off those ideas and feelings by throwing yourself wholeheartedly into your search. Sooner or later you will realise that the only thing you can really do is to let go with the flow of life. Let it take you wherever it wants, without expecting any rewards or results. You will see that only life is, only consciousness is, and that you don't exist as a separate entity, never did, and never will. That was just a temporary misunderstanding on your part, a fleeting dream in the all-inclusive mind of the totality of life.

How many of us have ever asked ourselves *who* or *what* it is that struggles so hard to attain something and if all the time, energy and money spent on the search ever actually lead anywhere? Even those of us who have asked such questions will tend to make all kinds of efforts to find the answers, progress along the spiritual path, and generally attempt to get somewhere, wherever that might be. By doing that, however, the mind is just trying to conquer or overcome itself, almost like a dog chasing its own tail, and sooner or later that will lead to disappointment and frustration, quite simply because it is an impossible task. But even that is perfectly all right, and in some ways a normal and even natural state of affairs.

The realisation of yourself as universal consciousness is the most natural and effortless thing in the world. It is not something that you can rush or force into being, and you don't need to either because you are already that. It really is as simple as this: You *are* the truth, just exactly the way you are right now. No more, no less. Once you have fully realised this, as a deep and immediate knowing, it is something that is always there, even if it might seem to recede into the background now and again. The peace that is beyond all understanding doesn't come and go, because it is exactly what you are; it is like the fragrance or flavour of your true nature.

If you don't know this, it is only because you have the mistaken idea that the truth somehow is other than you, or that you have to develop, purify or change yourself in some way to attain it. Moreover, there is no way you can ever define or describe your true nature, because any definition by its very nature imposes limitations. What you are is beyond all that, and can neither be quantified nor measured. It is infinite and eternal.

If you can let go of the notion that you are somebody, some particular person, separate from the totality of existence, any kind of split or duality within you will gradually dissolve. When you see all forms of life as nothing but ripples on the surface of the one eternal ocean of consciousness, you are indeed beginning to see life as it truly is. When peace and harmony manifest through you, conflicts seem to gradually fade away, quite simply because nothing outside of yourself exists. Everything just happens without anyone actually doing anything, or you could say that it is the totality of all life that is the ultimate mover and shaker.

What you are is neither an experience nor a state. It is beyond everything, yet intimately one with all. However, the desire for new experiences and special, mystical or expanded states of mind may well be the biggest obstacle to the realisation of your true nature. As long as you want to achieve something special, be someone special or want anything to last permanently, you are likely to remain ignorant of who you are, and thus more prone to ending up feeling frustrated. And even if you want to know how you can drop the wish for more and greater experiences or mystical states, you are no further forward because the motive behind such a question is exactly the same: you want, crave or desire something. Consequently, making a decision to relinquish all desire is absurd, precisely because it is desire itself that is the source of such a decision.

Your true nature is not something that comes and goes. It is always vitally alive here and now. If you think that you are separate from this all-embracing presence, you are mistaken. You cannot be separate from it, because you are it. Your true nature is not that of a separate little person or ego entity; it is unlimited, universal consciousness, plain and simple.

Everything that exists is the spontaneous expression of a creative, compassionate, intelligent, conscious presence of such order and magnitude that it is far beyond anything that the human mind can ever hope to comprehend. All the same, this supreme intelligence, this great spirit, is identical to what we are, and although our limited mind will never be able to understand it, let alone describe it, we are in fact always and forever one with it, whether we realise it or not.

As you will no doubt have heard or read previously, the cause of all suffering is precisely that one desires, wants something or is greedy, and there may be some truth in that. It is certainly the case that the desire for something to be different from what it is creates a kind of mental tension, which fuels the feeling of being a distinct entity. This separation is likely to be experienced as pain in one way or another, because it tends to shut you off from the very source of life itself.

We always seem to think that life can be different from what it is, but nothing can ever be anything else than what it is. Only this incessant creative outpouring of life in all its glory ever exists, and if you think otherwise, that is all just more illusion and make-believe, spontaneously manifesting in the eternal now of creation. There isn't necessarily anything wrong with daydreaming, flights of fancy and building castles in the air. On the contrary, it is quite all right. It may turn problematic only to the extent that we are identified with it or lost in it, which of course is what tends to happen more often than not.

Instead of living simply and naturally, most of us are involved in a desperate struggle to make life fit our own expectations, wishes and ideas. Needless to say, this brings disappointment, frustration and conflict. Disappointment because our expectations are rarely met, frustration because in the long run this is not very fulfilling, and conflict because there is almost always someone whose interests and wishes are contrary to our own. It does happen, of course, that life moves in accordance with one's desires, but the dubious kind of satisfaction this brings never lasts very long, because all things must pass.

Hoping that everything will become better tomorrow is a waste of energy as well as totally futile, and is nothing but a sophisticated form of escapism. Inventing the future has always been humanity's favourite way of getting away from it all. This is an absolutely infallible way of obscuring the reality of life as it is, but it has turned into a universal and deeply ingrained habit. Almost everybody continually fools themselves into believing that nothing is more natural and necessary than hoping for improved conditions tomorrow, but the fact is that nothing can improve in this manner, because tomorrow never comes. It is always today and life is always now. Haven't you noticed? And even if conditions do improve, it is not going to last. All forms are transitory, and all forms are destined to decay, break down, wither away and ultimately vanish without a trace. On the level of form, death is the only certainty, yet from the point of view of consciousness, which is the only point of view worthy of serious consideration, there is no death, only life. There is no time, only eternity. There is no space, only infinity. There is no separation, only oneness.

Most of us like to think that we know where we are going and how we are going to get there, thinking it is all going to lead to fulfilment and happiness somehow, someday, somewhere down the road, in the fullness of time, never realising that it is all a dream, just another little crinkly wrinkle in the infinite totality of consciousness. Well, maybe it is going to work out in our dreams after all, but that means precious little. Life always has its inscrutable ways of shattering all our dreams and fantasies, crushing our hopes and grinding our illusions down into the ground. Contrary to what most of us would instinctively say, this is very good news indeed, and exactly how it should and must be.

Whether we have materialistic desires or we are hankering for spiritual enlightenment is really all the same, because all illusions must come to an end sooner or later, as must everything else on the level of form. The ultimate illusion is of course the idea of a separate me, myself and I, yet it is only when the seeker has vanished or rather been seen never to have existed in the first place that the search finally has run its course, exhausted itself and come to an end. The search is over only when you realise that you never had any kind of reality as a separate entity and that the entire search was nothing more substantial than a swiftly forgotten dream about next to nothing at all. That is not the end of the journey though, but only the awakening to a new adventure; one which has neither beginning nor end.

The greatest enigma

A whole lot has been said and written about spiritual awakening over the years, but what does it all really mean? The way I see it, spiritual awakening is quite simply realising the truth of who you are. It means that you realise what your true identity is. Spiritual awakening is not necessarily an event that happens in time, at any particular place; it might just as well be a slow ripening of your understanding that seems to stretch across a period of many years. For some people, though, it is possible to talk of a before and after; a sudden, irreversible and sometimes even dramatic awakening to the truth of being.

The realisation of who you are in your essence is not really something that can be described as difficult or easy, because it is not a result of anything you can do or practise. The mystery of it is that it appears to happen of its own accord. It is like a plant slowly growing, flowering and bearing fruit. It is an effortless process, but because we usually see ourselves as separate and distinct entities it is often thought of as a personal achievement and something that requires sustained and arduous effort over a considerable amount of time.

It would be counterproductive to make the realisation of your true nature into a goal because it is not something that can be achieved by the ego, the limited somebody that most people take themselves to be. It is a completely natural flowering that is without cause and that cannot be explained. Once you know without a shadow of a doubt that you are pure, limitless, universal consciousness, you also realise that this is the beginning of a new journey, one without end, an adventure that has no goal and no other meaning than itself.

Hardly any of what is commonly thought of as spiritual practice, religious scripture and philosophical analysis has much bearing on the process of spiritual maturity. To the extent that you are interested in spiritual, religious and philosophical matters, you will come to know what it all means only when you know who you are. Before that, it is all stuff you can believe in or not, practise or not, but as far as spiritual awakening is concerned, it is neither relevant nor essential.

All forms of life quite spontaneously appear and disappear in consciousness. This includes the human brain and body, planet Earth, the universe and whatever else we usually think of as reality. Everything that we could ever think of as existing in time and space, as well as the very notion about time and space, are nothing but appearances, effortlessly rising and falling modulations in consciousness, drifting in and out of focus, a transitory dream show temporarily singing its song and dancing its dance only to disappear, never to be seen or heard from again. This never-ending creative and spontaneous outpouring is what we think of as life, and it is the effortless expression of an intelligence of such infinite creativity, magnitude and power that we will never even come close to a full understanding of it.

This conscious, creative, intelligent outpouring is eternally fresh and spontaneous. It is creativity on a level that is truly incomprehensible. It never repeats itself and always has plenty of surprises and unexpected twists and turns in store. If you are at all sensitive, you will already know that life often has the most exceptional ways of serving you something you hadn't expected, something you could never ever have imagined. Life is truly a blessing, a wonderful gift, and once you realise that you are not in charge of anything, you will more than likely just have a good laugh and enjoy the whole show. Then it is much easier to let go, relax and be open to the unknown, to let life take its course, safe in the knowledge that life is its own fulfilment, not really going anywhere, because there isn't anywhere to go. Life, energy, consciousness, being – it's all one, and you are that. Unconditional love is the natural and effortless flowering of that realisation.

But even so, even after realising your true nature as all-embracing eternal consciousness, you still have to face the many challenges that life is likely to throw your way. However transitory they may be, pain and pleasure are still intrinsic and unavoidable aspects of life. That's all right though and doesn't have to be a problem as long as we don't constantly try to run away from pain or chase after pleasure. Just trust in life and accept its bountiful gifts with grace and dignity.

You are not the doer. There is a much greater power instigating, moving and doing everything. It is not in any way separate from what is, rather it is the totality of all life and existence. Even though we might seem to be nothing but small parts in a much bigger picture, in essence we are life itself, always at one with the Great Spirit in which everything comes and goes. The Great Spirit is all; omnipresent, omnipotent and omniscient.

If you are not the doer, then what are you? If you look inside yourself, honestly and directly, what do you find? Are you able to find anyone there at all? There is the thought and feeling of me, the person, the ego with all its history and experiences, but all of that seems rather flimsy if you really try to get to the core of it.

If you don't think about anything and let go of the notion of the separate self for a moment, you'll soon realise that there is nothing there; it's just an infinite emptiness without a real centre. Maybe you think that this sounds very negative and somewhat empty of substance, but if you go into it, you will eventually realise that it is also the ultimate fullness. There is nothing here other than universal consciousness taking on ever new forms. That's all. You are not separate from the Great Spirit, All That Is, Universal Consciousness, God or whatever words you want to use. You are that, whether you are ready to see and accept it or not.

When all is said and done, isn't it a question of what it is that is aware of all this here now? And also, where does the impulse to awakening come from in the first place? It's clearly not anything to do with the mind-based egocentric entity. It goes much deeper than that, but I doubt that anyone will ever be able to explain it.

Moreover, does awakening happen spontaneously? Is it without cause? Is it something like amazing grace? Do awareness, presence, consciousness arise from awareness itself? Does presence of being arise from being itself? If so, does this mean that consciousness all of a sudden becomes interested in itself? And if so, where does that impulse come from? Why now, why here, how come, and for what purpose? I'm throwing all these questions at you in the hope that you will stop, let them in and consider them very deeply. Sometimes it's good to ask seemingly impossible questions like that even if you have no hope of ever getting any answers. Just bear in mind that it's not really about getting answers that can be verbalised, conceptualised and debated. Much more important than that is the process of enquiry that you automatically nourish when you ask impossible questions and questions that may not even have any answers. That in itself will have a much greater impact on your journey of awakening than any theory, belief or clever intellectual answers can ever have.

While it may seem as if this book appears to supply a fair few answers, none of these answers are meant as absolute and unassailable truths that are set in stone forevermore. Whatever answers I may present in this book can at best be thought of as nourishing little nibbles to sustain you on a journey that is much more profound and meaningful than any cleverly expressed theory or verbal statement can ever be. And in any case, I would strongly suggest that you consistently make every possible effort to question all answers, regardless of where you may come across them.

What is it that makes self-realisation happen to somebody?

How come certain people somehow seem to wake up from their spiritual sleep? It appears to be a totally incomprehensible mystery, but maybe the question itself doesn't really make sense. After all, spiritual awakening must necessarily be as natural and effortless as nature waking up again when spring arrives, or the flowers opening themselves to the rays of sunshine each morning.

The realisation of who you are has nothing to do with anything that you can ever do or practise, neither is it connected to any method, religious beliefs and discipline or anything like that. It makes no difference whether you are a saint or a sinner, a good person or a bad person, rich or poor, famous or somebody totally unknown. If it happens, it happens. If it doesn't, it doesn't – or at least not just yet. That's about as much as anyone can say about it.

On the other hand, nobody can avoid the realisation of their true nature forever, so there's no need to worry about it. You can't avoid it and you can't hurry it, that's all. Just bear in mind that it's never wise to try and pick a fruit before it is ripe, so save yourself the frustration of even trying. Instead of trying to force what is essentially a completely natural and effortless process, consider the possibility of quite simply saying a big "YES" to the totality of life, just the way it is. This means that you stop fighting with what is already the case, accept what is here now and let everything be as it is.

However, do bear in mind that this doesn't mean that you become a passive spectator to life and whatever it brings you. If you find yourself in a sticky mess, it is of course natural and justified to take the necessary steps to get out of it, just as a cat would jump out of the water and rather bask lazily in the sunshine. What's important is that you let go of the inner resistance to the aspects of life that might not feel so great. You surrender totally to whatever happens while also effortlessly doing what needs to be done at any particular time, in whatever situation you might find yourself. Just let go with the flow, enjoy the show, and learn to laugh at the absurdity of your own efforts.

And if you think all of this sounds just too frustrating and not very helpful at all, you may indeed find a way forward if you let this good old Zen saying be your guiding light for a while: "Sitting silently, doing nothing. Spring comes and the grass grows by itself."

A case of mistaken identity

It should be abundantly clear by now that in my opinion the most important question you can ever ask yourself is this: "Who am I?" On the journey of spiritual awakening, this is the most fundamental question of all, because if you haven't figured out who or what you are, then what good could anything else ever be? After all, your own existence is the only thing you can never doubt no matter how hard you might try. You may question absolutely everything, and rightfully so, but the fact that you do exist is something that is pretty hard to explain away. It is both illogical and absurd to doubt that you are, because in the first place you have to exist in order to doubt or question anything at all.

The only thing that any of us can ever say with absolute certainty is this: "I am." That's all. It can also be expressed quite simply and maybe even more accurately as, "Consciousness is," or even, "There is conscious experience," but irrespective of how you verbalise it, it's really the only objectively true statement that you can ever make. Everything else is either conjecture, only relatively true, taken on blind faith or just hearsay, gossip and tittle-tattle.

However, if you ask yourself just verbally what or who you are, and think that doing this will get you anything in particular, whether you think you are going to reach heaven, nirvana, enlightenment or whatever else you might fancy, you will never get to the root of it. If there is any kind of motive behind the question other than an inner compulsion to know what your true nature is, it becomes just another method to reach some goal in the future, and will only keep you stuck in the same old rut. You have to be genuinely passionate about finding out what you are, to the point of feeling consumed by it, maybe even obsessed, because only then will you be able to find a way into this enquiry that will work for you. This is of course nothing that can be cultivated, because it has to arise naturally and spontaneously from within you. Only then is it truly authentic.

I have already made statements to the effect that what you are, what we all are, is quite simply consciousness, but just hearing or reading that is unlikely to make much difference to you unless you are able to see the truth of it directly for yourself. Therefore, the question "Who am I?" isn't one that can conveniently be answered on the level of mind and thought. You have to know it, embody it and make it a reality in your experience, because only then will it make any difference. Otherwise, whatever answers the conditioned mind dreams up, can at best only be pointers to truth, and are likely to be distractions more than anything else.

So how can you approach this most fundamental and essential quest in a way that is both practical and effective? I would suggest that you start by deeply and seriously considering something that is actually blatantly obvious, but for the most part completely overlooked or ignored. It is the most basic truth of all, and I will try to put it into as simple terms as possible:

You know without a doubt that you have been through all sorts of experiences and adventures during your life. You have known success and failure, you have won and lost, and you have tried, failed and tried time and time again, sometimes meeting with great success, at other times not. During the course of your lifetime you have come to know a wide spectrum of human emotions and experiences, and something has always been going on inside you and all around you. It is an undeniable fact that experiences, sensations and all the rest of it come and go, thoughts and feelings appear and disappear, wakefulness, sleep, birth and death come and go, but throughout all of this there is one constant that never ever changes.

That one constant is the obvious fact that you are; the self-evident truth of your being, which is consciousness itself. The eternal unchanging consciousness that you are is the screen on which all possible dramas are acted out. Everything that appears to be happening in this world, or any other world for that matter, is truly nothing but forms appearing and disappearing in consciousness. It is consciousness modulating itself into ever new shapes and experiences, yet always being exactly what it always is.

The only thing that has been constant throughout everything that you have ever entangled yourself in and out of, the only thing which has never ever changed is precisely what you are – the being that you are. You have always been there, no matter what has happened to you. You have been there as the constant awareness of all change. Throughout all the ups and downs and the perpetual change that life always brings, the consciousness that you are holds everything in its silent embrace. This is an obvious fact, although not that many people seem to know that or understand the significance of it, in fact most people have probably never given any of this much thought at all.

The bare fact of your existence – *consciousness itself* – is indisputable, self-evident and unshakable. You can of course have all sorts of thoughts, theories, explanations and feelings about all this, and you most probably will, but none of that can ever change the fact that you are. Whatever is happening, whether it is internally or externally – you are always there as the awareness that envelops it all. This awareness, which is what you are beyond thoughts, feelings, personality and all the rest of it, is always completely non-judgemental and totally accepting of everything that ever happens. It cannot be defined or described, as it is not an object that can be externalised. It is quite simply the formless dimension in which all phenomena come and go. It just is, and without it nothing on the level of form could ever exist. Just as the empty endlessness of the sky cannot be touched or affected by the clouds drifting by, the universal consciousness that you are is in essence completely untouched and unaffected by anything that drifts past on this journey we call life.

There isn't actually anything you can do directly to realise this. It's not a question of practising anything, disciplining yourself, renouncing or adding anything. Either you see the truth of this or you don't. If you don't see it now, that's perfectly all right, because sooner or later you will, and then you will also know that realising the truth of your being is not a result of anything you can ever do. There is no technique, method or system that will ever lead to the realisation of the fundamental truth of what you are. The various methods and systems of meditation, yoga, self-development and so on that have been devised throughout history are certainly good enough for their own purposes, whatever those might be, so I'm not suggesting that anyone should stop practising any method or technique they find useful or enjoyable.

However, all methods are quite frankly irrelevant when it comes to knowing what you essentially are. The reason for that is that the essence of being is already the case; it is obvious, unarguable and irrefutable. Nothing can be added to it and nothing can be taken away from it. It is the formless reality that underlies all external forms, the one consciousness that is nothing and everything at the same time.

Everything that seems to exist does so only by virtue of consciousness, which holds the world, the universe and whatever else there might be within its formless embrace. Nothing is external to the universal creative intelligent conscious awareness that is all, yet it is itself dependent on nothing. It is all, yet completely untouched by any of the innumerable forms that constantly appear within it. What you are is all-embracing universal consciousness, everything that appears to you appears within consciousness, and indeed everything that ever appears on the level of form is just another modulation of consciousness.

You may wonder if consciousness is some sort of a thing or a certain something that can be described, defined, categorised or pigeonholed in some way, but this is of course not the case at all. All definitions, descriptions and ways of categorising will by their very nature be imposing limitations, and no limitations can ever be put on that which is eternal and infinite, beyond time and space. Consciousness is beyond what the mind can grasp, understand or relate to. It is completely formless, beyond time and space, it is never born and it never dies, yet it holds everything within itself and expresses itself as everything. Everything depends on consciousness, yet it does not depend on anything. Let the whole of external existence vanish, and consciousness remains what it is. And that is what you are.

Now ask yourself this simple question: "What is it that is aware of these words and their meaning?" If you go deeply into this question you will find that consciousness itself is aware, or maybe you could say that awareness is conscious. Whether we say that awareness is aware of itself, or that consciousness is conscious of itself, it means the same thing. The point is that there is no such thing as a separate entity or person that is aware or conscious; there is only consciousness, awareness, being.

You might think that this sounds somewhat implausible, or much too simplified, and that's fair enough and certainly a valid view. However, if you explore this and give your whole life to find the truth of it, you will realise that there is no individual, separate self to be found at all, and that the limited ego-self with its history and baggage is only a temporary and ultimately fictitious entity. That make-believe self is only yet another object appearing and disappearing in consciousness, and while it does of course seem to exist, it does so only as a purely functional entity expressed as an ego with a distinct personality, with its likes and dislikes, peculiarities and idiosyncrasies. This entity, which is what most people mistakenly take as their real self, is ultimately an illusion, of no more substance than a fleeting shadow across a distant hillside. Regardless of what happens or doesn't happen, whatever we think we are doing or not doing, all that ever happens is the one universal consciousness expressing itself as the many, the formless manifesting as form, so there is no need to take any of it personally.

It is almost universally assumed and accepted that every one of us is a separate entity engaged in real activities in a real world. This is an assumption that is hardly ever questioned or scrutinised by anyone, maybe because it seems so obvious that it must be so. After all, everybody behaves and speaks in a way that only reinforces this notion of separateness, so even though we may be at odds with each other in many ways and disagree on many issues, the idea of separate beings is implicitly taken for granted by virtually everybody. In fact, this idea is so ingrained in us that most people would probably think you are a bit strange, maybe even off your rocker and totally nuts, if you were to suggest that this might not necessarily be the case.

We are used to defining ourselves and our identity in many different ways, such as in terms of age, religion, political affiliation, social position, career and so on. Even one's name functions as a kind of marker of identity. However, even the most cursory investigation into the matter of identity will soon reveal to anyone who's just a little bit persistent that all such labels are quite irrelevant when it comes to discovering the actual nature of who you are. Anyone who sincerely asks themselves the simple question "Who am I?" will sooner or later realise that their most fundamental identity is not to be found in anything that has been accumulated through cultural influences, upbringing, religious or political conditioning and so on. And as for the circumstances you were born into, such as race, nationality, ethnicity, gender or family, there is no home for your essential identity there either.

A sincere and persistent quest to find out what you are will sooner or later lead you to the inescapable conclusion that you are nothing rather than something, nobody rather than somebody, which just means that what you are can't be defined within the context and limited framework of space and time. In other words, what you are is beyond form; your true nature is infinite, eternal, formless and timeless. It is without definable attributes. There is obviously consciousness, awareness, being, but is this something that is separate from existence itself? You will hopefully already have come to the conclusion that the answer to that question is quite simply: No. You are the Great Spirit, universal consciousness, formless being, expressing itself through body, mind and personality within the confines of a world that is ultimately just about as substantial as the world you encounter in your night-time dreams.

The formless presence that you are is not personal in the sense of being separate from anything else. It is quite simply the underlying reality of everything that appears on the level of form, and the foundation of everything we know as the world and the universe. Form and formless are not separate, in fact it would be more accurate to say that form is the formless and that the formless is form. To simplify this more than we probably should, you could say that universal consciousness is separate from the manifest world only in the sense that it is completely unaffected or untouched by what is happening on the level of form, but on the other hand it is equally true to say that the manifest world is nothing but the externalised expression of formless consciousness.

Once you realise that you are formless, timeless consciousness, the way you relate to other people and the circumstances of life will start to be transformed. The reason for this is that you will realise that other people and the circumstances of life, and indeed the world itself, are not different from or external to you. They are what you are. It is all the same supremely creative intelligence expressing itself through an infinite variety of forms. This also means that it doesn't really matter that much what happens on the level of form, because all forms are destined to vanish, and that does of course include the forms you know as your body, mind and personality. Death isn't a calamity that we need to be afraid of. It is just a natural part of life, and whether or not a particular form lives or dies is at the end of the day not all that important.

You may feel inclined to ask if such a way of looking at life and identity could lead to cynicism, lack of empathy, or even callousness, and that would certainly be a fair question. It might seem like a reasonable conclusion to what you have just read, but the exact opposite is a lot more likely to be the case. Somebody who has realised his or her true nature as pure, unlimited, formless consciousness, will also experience a heightened capacity for love, empathy, care and compassion for others and the world. When you know your true nature, you also know that you are all, so being in conflict with others or with the world is no longer a very attractive proposition, in fact it becomes quite impossible, because you realise that there are no others to be in conflict with. To put it simply, unconditional love is the fragrance of the flowering of spiritual realisation.

But even if you think that all of this sounds fine and dandy, bona fide and above board, you might still be wondering how it can ever make any real difference to anybody's life. After all, to a lot of people this might seem like nothing more than theoretical musings about things that are of interest only to people who like to be engrossed in metaphysical speculation and obscure philosophical matters. Fair enough, it could well be that this is of interest only to people who are somewhat philosophically inclined, but realising who you are does make a big difference, in fact it is the most important and life-changing realisation you can ever have. The realisation of one's essential being as consciousness itself has far-reaching consequences, not least because it has the potential of changing the world for the better beyond all recognition.

Virtually every single problem facing humanity today is rooted in the erroneous assumption that we are all separate beings living in an objectively real world stuffed full of something called physical matter believed to exist independently of consciousness. That is where the basic flaw, the fundamental misunderstanding and the original sin all reside. What we are looking at is really nothing more than a case of mistaken identity, but it is a very serious case because of the devastating and catastrophic consequences. If you experience yourself as being separate, you will of necessity also feel a need to fight for your survival, and more often than not at somebody else's expense, which means that you will be in a state of conflict with others. A separate ego will more often than not be at odds with other separate egos, and this is the seed of every single conflict and war we have ever known and experienced.

Peace, harmony, freedom and love can only ever be a universally experienced reality once we see through the illusion of ego and separateness and start to live from a perspective of oneness, from the unshakeable conviction that our true identity is nothing less than universal, limitless consciousness. That's what's needed for the new humanity on a new Earth to become a living reality. We can of course carry on with our endless struggles to create peaceful relations between peoples and nations. We can continue our many ways of deceiving ourselves by thinking that peace prizes and so-called peacekeeping forces can ever make any difference. We can keep on engaging in all our numerous other attempts at making efforts to create a better, more peaceful Earth, but the question is: Does any of it ever help to create a better and more peaceful world? It may seem so in the short run, but the truth of the matter is that none of these efforts and activities can ever do anything to remove the real cause of all the world's conflicts and suffering.

Only authentic self-knowledge and the love that effortlessly flows from that will ever make a difference. This is what it's going to take, and no authority or government in the world has or can ever have any kind of control over this process. In fact, governments, authorities and legislators, wherever they may be in the world, all seem to be totally clueless about this. That is quite obviously the case, because it is by the fruit of their actions that we can tell whether they act from a state of ignorance or wisdom. And sadly, it is only too obvious that world leaders, politicians and other people of influence are overwhelmingly driven by desire and fear, just like most of the rest of us.

We have to stop expecting somebody else to put things right in the world. Creating peace on Earth and a world of love and harmony is entirely up to you out there somewhere reading this, and you need to realise that it is your personal responsibility to make this into a living reality. The world is not different or foreign to what you are. You are the world, and whether you live in conflict or harmony, you will unfailingly have a direct effect on what the world is. But please don't feel intimidated by any of this. If you see the truth of it, you will soon meet this challenge with delight. Let unconditional love be your guiding light, and thereby you will be a true blessing to all life.

What is life?

In our culture it is universally accepted and taken for granted by nearly everybody that the three-dimensional world of matter is the ultimate bedrock of reality and that it all exists independently of the observer. Have you ever seriously considered the possibility that this might not be the case? Have you ever asked yourself if what we usually think of as life and reality might not be quite as real as we usually think it is? Have you ever wondered if it might be closer to the truth to compare life to a dream? I think it was Einstein who once said that the universe is an illusion, albeit a very persistent one. I might be paraphrasing the great man, but you get the idea.

If you have ever been fortunate enough to ask yourself questions like these, you might also have felt at times as if you are nothing but a character in a play or a movie or some silly soap opera. You may have felt as if you are just playing a part, acting out the drama, the passion, the tragedy, the comedy and absurdity of it all. You're going through the motions if you like. Just have a look at what you're doing now for example; you might be sitting somewhere reading these words, with a number of other things happening around you, but where does it all come from? You don't actually plan or decide that any of this should happen, and even if you think you do, then who or what is doing the deciding? The fictional self that most people think they are has no power to decide or do anything, precisely because it is a fictional entity. The limited ego-self might well seem to be eminently functional and useful on a practical level, but it's not ultimately real.

There isn't really a person as such anywhere, or you could say that the personality is something that you wear like a mask or costume, when interacting with the world, but apart from that, you are nothing, emptiness, no self if you like. Another way of looking at it is to say that you are awareness or consciousness, or maybe just being. That awareness, or being, is not ultimately personal. There is only ever the one expressing itself as the many, so in that sense we are all exactly the same, only expressed in different ways, appearing in different and ever-changing disguises. You might have many clothes and outfits in your wardrobe, but none of them can ever change what you truly are. All forms are expressions of the same source, which we may think of as universal, intelligent, creative consciousness. It is the Great Spirit giving birth to itself in the form of an external world, the formless emerging as form, nothingness appearing as somethingness.

When this starts to dawn on you, it can be pretty unnerving, as if everything starts falling apart. You could easily end up in a state in which nothing of what you held dear and thought was real stands up for scrutiny anymore, and nothing much seems to make a lot of sense. On the other hand, after realising the truth of what you are, you might actually feel that everything makes perfect sense and you feel totally at ease with it all.

In any case, somewhere along the way you are likely to realise that all values, morality and norms accepted by society are completely false, nothing more than arbitrary conventions, that it is all just one big performance, a curious mixture of comedy, tragedy, drama, pathos, playfulness and absurdity. We have all heard or read that all the world is a stage and that everyone is just playing their parts, and there's a lot of truth in that. However, if you take the performance seriously and think it is real, then you are making life more difficult than it has to be, quite simply because it isn't ultimately real, only relatively so. What we think of as life can, with a bit of poetic licence, be described as a dream in God's mind. It's a very convincing dream for sure, but a dream nonetheless, in which the seemingly separate characters all take themselves to be real entities in an objectively existing reality. To quote the Bard again, "we are all such stuff as dreams are made on" and it's all "much ado about nothing".

You could also use the metaphor of a movie or theatre performance to get closer to realising that life may not be quite what we think it is. You might feel emotionally engaged when you watch a movie, but you don't honestly think that it's real, that what you see on screen is actually happening, do you? You can be watching the most heart-wrenching drama, but even if somehow you could step into it, you wouldn't be able to take it seriously, because you would know that the actors are just that – actors, just pretending, playing their parts. Good actors can do that sort of thing very convincingly, so we tend to suspend our better judgement about it while watching a well-made movie or a great play at the theatre, but underneath that we still know that it's just acting, that none of it is actually happening for real.

Now consider what it must feel like to have the same unshakeable knowing about *this* so-called reality: Try to imagine that what we usually refer to as life is nothing more than a dream or a staged play. Just picture it: You can see very clearly that everything is just a dream, or like a movie, with actors playing their various parts. There is not a shadow of doubt in your mind that this is actually how it is, and everything, including all aspects of your own life, is just about as substantial as little puffs of steam vanishing into thin air. Once you get to that stage, it is really hard to feel any kind of belonging or connection to any of it, isn't it?

You don't really feel caught up in it like you once did, and once you are in that position, you just cannot take any of it seriously anymore. It becomes impossible because you realise that success and failure, gain and loss, fortune and adversity, health and sickness, birth and death, and whatever else you might encounter, all truly amount to exactly the same; precisely nothing. They are all apparitions or appearances in consciousness, and regardless of what happens or doesn't happen, what you really are behind it all is the only constant, the one thing that never changes or disappears.

If everything seems to you like it is a dream, you are also likely to feel somewhat estranged from the so-called normal world in a peculiar kind of way. If this has happened to you or if it ever should happen to you, you are likely to feel as if you don't belong to this world anymore, or certainly not to the world that is considered real by the vast majority of people. Even though it might not feel real or important to you anymore, it's still a good idea to do the best you can in whatever circumstances you might find yourself, because that is just the most natural and practical way of dealing with the ups and downs of life. There is nothing to lose, you are already saved by virtue of your very existence, and regardless of what might happen on your journey through life, you instinctively know that it's all right. Whatever is happening, or appears to be happening, is just another dreamlike storyline, and therefore it's not that important, at least not in the ultimate sense.

You may well be in this world, but you're ultimately not of it. After all, what you essentially are does not depend on this world or anything in it. The universal consciousness that you are is the ultimate reality, whereas the society we appear to be a part of, our entire civilisation for that matter, is nothing more than a flimsy dream, for the most part built on utterly false values and pretentious make-believe. Once you have stepped on to the road less travelled and seen the truth of who you are, you will never again be able to convince yourself that this mad, sad, hilarious and beautiful world is your true home, but you won't mind. You can still move about in the world and appear to be doing all sorts of things, just like any other average little bumpkin out there. Maybe you feel a bit awkward about it, but you will soon realise that it's perfectly all right. Even if you might be in a different dimension altogether, hardly anyone will ever notice unless you accidentally or intentionally break their arbitrary rules of morality and decorum. After all, if it's all only like a play, a movie or a dream, then it doesn't matter that much anyway, does it? It's no big deal anymore.

Anyone who lives in peace and harmony lives in accordance with the wholeness of life, and then everything is right just the way it is. There's no need to worry about right and wrong, because nothing can ever be different from what it is. Right and wrong, good and bad, are only ideas about what is, not absolute values or truths. All divisions are ultimately illusory, so doing any kind of harm to anyone or anything is just absurd, and something that you would never even consider as an option. Everybody and everything, all forms of life spring from the same inexhaustible, eternal source, and anyone who has realised this is a blessing to the world, even those few who, for whatever reason, live the life of a reclusive hermit in some remote location far away from the hustle and bustle, noise and madness of the world.

The basic reality of all forms is universal consciousness, because that's ultimately what everything is made from, and what makes the perceived world appear as real. What we are is all one, without any divisions anywhere. Understanding and living this is the basis of all true morality and ethics, and that's all you really need. It has nothing to do with society's norms and values, laws, rules and regulations, which more often than not have been born from a self-centred state of conflict and disharmony.

While it may be true that humanity isn't yet mature enough for a world without an enormous number of laws, rules and regulations to keep society functioning at all, it is also equally true that in a world inhabited by people who effortlessly live in peace, love and harmony, there is no need for arbitrary man-made rules and regulations and the maddening and often frustrating bureaucracy that necessarily follows. Other than the Highway Code and suchlike, it's all completely redundant in a world made from love. To the spiritually awake humanity, there are no others, we are all the same universal self, and selfless love is the natural and effortless expression of that realisation. For the blessed people inhabiting the new Earth, that will be the only moral or ethical guideline that anyone will ever need.

You might think that this all sounds a bit far-fetched and unrealistic, but if it seems utopian that's only because the present state of affairs with all its conflicts and disharmony is so universally prevalent that we think it's just how it has to be. It has often been said that what the world needs is love, and while this is obviously true, it is only selfless love that can ever make a difference, but then that's the only real love there ever is. This love flows effortlessly from the realisation of one's true nature as infinite and eternal consciousness, and this is the only thing that can ever make any difference in this matter. And that realisation is what we usually call spiritual awakening.

It is also worth mentioning that within the context of a spiritually mature way of life one's ethics and moral standards are of crucial importance. That doesn't mean that one has to adhere to specific rules and guidelines of ethics, but rather that one's level of spiritual maturity is reflected in how one treats other people. All too often I have come across people who on the surface seem to be very spiritual and committed to what they think of as their spiritual growth, yet at the same time acting in ways which are utterly selfish and ego-centred.

This is unfortunately also the case for certain spiritual teachers operating within the contemporary spiritual marketplace. They might argue that their teaching is expressed through something they euphemistically like to call "crazy wisdom", but that is an oxymoron if ever there was one. Crazy is crazy, wisdom is wisdom, and never the twain shall meet.

The proliferation of people setting themselves up as spiritual teachers lately is perhaps not that surprising, but it seems to me that only a minority of the teachers who talk about spirituality nowadays have something to offer beyond mere platitudes and clichés. Has it become all too easy to jump on the spiritual teacher bandwagon and get the admiration and adulation of spiritual seekers? All of this is whatever it is and neither right nor wrong of course, but it does beg the question: "How many spiritual teachers does it take to screw in a light bulb?" I shall leave you to ponder that and find the answer for yourself.

After all is said and done, one's spirituality is measured solely on the grounds of one's ability to treat other people with love, kindness and generosity, and thus manifest unconditional love in the world. If that is not demonstrably in place, it really doesn't matter how much so-called work one does on oneself, how many spiritual experiences one has, how many ascended masters one has had a chat with, how many past lives one can remember or how spiritually advanced one thinks one is. All of that is irrelevant if the ethics and morality of one's life are not built on the rock solid foundation of unconditional love. Let love and a genuinely heart-centred approach to ethics guide your life, and you won't need to worry about your level of spirituality anymore.

So, in light of the above, what is life? There are many ways of answering that question, and no verbal answer will ever manage to capture the essence of it. We can hopefully all agree that life is a precious gift and a beautiful blessing, and that it is ultimately a great and glorious mystery. And thus it has been said that life is not a problem to be solved, but a mystery to be lived, which I think is a beautiful way of putting it. Quite simply put, life is all. There is nothing that is not life, and death is just a transformation of form. It's all part of life. Only life is. Life is universal consciousness, which is supreme intelligence and creativity. Life takes on many forms, yet in its essence always remains life.

You can't think yourself to reality, and no mental construct or system of thought can ever capture the truth of what life is. All religion, theology, philosophy, ideology as well as all of science are constructs of thought, and as such can be more or less useful and interesting, but none of these can capture and reveal the essence of life itself. Reality can only be revealed to you once you go beyond all these man-made conceptual constructions, beyond all forms, beyond all theories and systems of thought, to the placeless place where consciousness alone is. Then you will see that all systems of thought, as well as everything else are all nothing but appearances in and manifestations of consciousness. And that essential consciousness is what you are.

Go through life as if you are not the one who is the doer, but rather as if everything just happens, even when you appear to be making a decision to do something. Nobody is actually doing anything, and this writing is just happening, just as the reading of it is just happening. What is it that is conscious of it all?

See yourself as totally transparent, as limitless emptiness without a centre. Just be the open space in which the forms and events of life are allowed to come and go. Can you be that space? It hardly makes a difference whether you believe you can or not, because all your beliefs are purely on the level of mind and do not make a jot of difference to what is here now, although they are certainly part of the form that life is presently taking. All of what appears to you as life is contained within the consciousness that you are, so be knowingly the emptiness that is the ultimate fullness.

Universal consciousness, supreme intelligence, all that is, the Great Spirit, God, the Source – these are all just words, yet pointing to something so beautiful, vast, incomprehensible, incredible, mysterious and utterly miraculous that no words can ever represent or express it. What is it? We know it as life, but it is not just the many forms of life; it is form and formless, being and nothingness, one and all, everything and nothing. The only thing we can say with certainty is that it alone is. It is all that is, as currently expressed in the eternal now, and this is it.

The mystery of life

Have you ever wondered what the meaning of life is? Well, in case you haven't already figured it out, I'll tell you straight away. The meaning of life is life itself. To search for or imagine any other meaning is pointless because life has no need for any kind of meaning external to itself. It is its own meaning, purpose and fulfilment. It doesn't need any other explanation, definition or clarification, and whatever anyone could possibly say about life and its meaning will at best be somewhat inadequate. Life is all there ever is. Life is creative, compassionate, intelligent consciousness. It is the Great Spirit spontaneously manifesting on the level of form, yet always and forever resting in its own perfection.

You must figure all of this out for yourself though, because it's no good just reading it here, or listening to somebody else telling you this. If it comes from somebody else or you read it in a book such as this one, it's just another piece of information that you will accept or reject according to your particular conditioning. It is absolutely essential that you find whatever answers you need for yourself, through your own experience, and thus the truth will indeed set you free once you do know it.

But do we really want to know the truth? Most of us would probably say we are all for truth, and that's an easy game to play if we see truth as something abstract, or something to play around with in the dimension of ideas and beliefs. But if truth should happen to open our eyes to what petty, shallow and pitiful lives we often live, then it's not so easy anymore, is it? Living a make-believe and superficial life seems to be the rule rather than the exception these days, and it may well be an easy way out, but it's hardly satisfying in the long run. If we are at all honest with ourselves, truth is for the most part something we just don't want to know about if it challenges or destroys our self-image and the belief systems we have so carefully constructed over many years.

Many of us tend to end up as second-hand people who just accept what we are told by anyone in authority. Instead of finding things out for ourselves and exploring the inexhaustible mystery of life through our own experience, we look up to whatever authorities we believe in and expect them to tell us what is right and wrong, what we ought to do and what the meaning of life is. It's not terribly difficult to deceive ourselves into believing that we are seeking the truth, but if we are to be just a little bit honest with ourselves, we will have to admit that most of the time we just want to escape from it all, and whether we do that through materialistic or religious means is all rather irrelevant.

It is all too common just to accept whatever the so-called experts have told us about any given subject, whether it's something philosophical and religious or to do with more mundane matters. Consider all the things you currently accept as fact, truth or scientifically proven, and then ask yourself: "Do I really know that this is the truth?" If you make a diligent and honest effort to find the truth about anything, you may be surprised to discover that many of those things that you have been told and taught over the years often have very little to do with what is actually true, but more to do with the kind of endemic conditioning, indoctrination and brainwashing that is so prevalent in our society. Isn't it often the case that a so-called truth is nothing but a lie repeated so many times and so often that we have started to believe that it certainly must be true?

The great American author and humourist Mark Twain is reported to have said: *"It is much easier to fool people than to convince them that they have been fooled."* There is a lot of life experience and wisdom in that statement, because once we have accepted something as true, regardless of whether it is something our religious or spiritual authorities have told us or it is something that we have constantly heard repeated via mass media or education, we will often find it very difficult to change our minds about it. The reason for that of course is that it hurts to admit, even just to ourselves, that we have been tricked, misled and duped.

When reading statements like those above, it's possible that you may think to yourself: "That's all very well and maybe it's the case for most people, but I am a very spiritual person, so I'm not like that." If your attitude is anything at all like that, you're definitely travelling along the path of self-deception. Taking refuge in religion, spirituality, philosophy and suchlike often doesn't make much of a difference. Elevating a certain teaching, religion or guru into an authority is nothing more than a cop-out, however advanced it may seem to be. When it comes to self-knowledge and spiritual awakening, only your own authentic experience and genuine understanding can ever make any real difference. Question everything! Put all answers up for scrutiny, and accept nothing unless you know through your own experience that it is true. Only then will you be fully understanding it, living it, breathing it, digesting it. Only then will you know the truth, and only then will it set you free.

In order to know who you are, it is important that you let go of any attachment to your opinions and prejudices, your intellectual knowledge and whatever you may happen to believe in. Letting go of your attachment to the information you have so carefully collected over many years can be painful and is often a process that could stretch across years or even decades. Nevertheless, isn't it obvious that theoretical knowledge can be one of the greatest obstacles if you want to know the truth of who you are and what life is? At the very least, you have to be open to the possibility that you might be ignorant about everything that really matters. It's after all a lot better to be ignorant and know that for a fact than to be ignorant, and possibly even stupid, yet think that you know it all.

And when it comes to waking up to the truth of what you are, none of your opinions, knowledge and training has much of a relevance anyway. However, what really does matter, if you want to know the truth of who you are, is quite simply just your burning passion for truth. If that is the most important thing in your life, then you will know the truth and the truth will indeed set you free. In the quest for truth, all superfluous baggage must be left behind. You have to learn to explore life without constantly comparing, analysing, judging, rejecting or accepting, and blindly believing in this, that or the other. In other words, freedom from the known must be your point of departure, not your goal.

Many people will never even consider the possibility that they might be ignorant about their true identity, primarily because that wouldn't do much to boost their sense of ego and self-importance. All the same, it is reasonable to suggest that most people seem to be in a state of deep sleep, and I am talking about a kind of spiritual sleep of course. The problem is that hardly anyone realises that they are indeed fast asleep. We are all constantly busy trying to achieve this, that or the other in life, but whether one ever achieves anything or not on one's journey through life, it is much more important to realise and acknowledge one's own state of spiritual poverty. That's often what is required to ignite a passionate and authentic quest for truth, or in the words of Christian scripture: "Blessed are the poor in spirit, for theirs is the Kingdom of Heaven." In other words, if, like Socrates, you know that you know nothing, you are much more likely to stumble upon the truth of who you are and what life is.

You probably don't need me to tell you that there is a lot more to life than just falling asleep in front of the idiot-box every evening, and otherwise slaving yourself to death in a rotten rat-race in which the rewards are stress, mounting debt and continuous worrying about just about everything. Incredible as it seems, a lot of people accept such a way of life without ever questioning it. Apparently, we also seem to think that it is some kind of law of nature that life has to be a hopeless and futile struggle for survival. We fight our way through each day, all the time struggling to keep up appearances, generally trying to maintain our illusions about what wholesome and meaningful lives we are living. In order to avoid having to confront our own inner emptiness, many of us have a tendency to fill our lives with as much activity, things, possessions and people as possible. A typical approach to life nowadays seems to consist of workaholism, cheap entertainment, an impressive array of electronic gadgets and getting intoxicated by alcohol or drugs as often as one can.

A disproportionate amount of our time and energy is spent on escapism in one form or another. We gorge ourselves on TV, radio, newspapers, magazines, books, movies, theatre, music, sports, gambling, drugs, sex and whatever else we can grab hold of as soon as we get even the slightest sense of the bottomless void inside us. And I'm not so sure that those of us who, for whatever reason, have religious and spiritual inclinations are any better off. There are millions of people all over the world who use meditation, yoga, prayer, occultism, spiritualism and religious rituals to escape from the stark truth about their own lives. This may be slightly more sophisticated than drinking oneself into a mindless stupor, but fundamentally it amounts to the same.

If somehow all the mechanisms of escape we are all so fond of were to be removed at a stroke – whether it is the pious Sunday sermons delivered by the priests, legal and illegal drugs, the inane and ridiculous blathering of politicians, ideologues and demagogues, television's relentless and stupefying brainwashing, all sorts of pointless toys and gadgets, constantly adding to our cherished collection of things and memories, all the witless balderdash that newspapers and magazines are always overflowing with – the result would more than likely be massive panic and total chaos.

Please don't think that I am against creative pursuits and all the other activities that inevitably form the fabric of our lives. All creative expression is wonderful, and life would be impossible without it, quite simply because life itself is the ultimate expression of creativity. So being creative and actively pursuing our many interests and goals can be both fulfilling and rewarding, and there isn't intrinsically anything wrong with any of it, or at least not as long as it doesn't do any harm to others or to the blessed Earth. However, I still contend that it is an obvious fact that we tend to spend an awful lot of time, energy and money trying to escape from ourselves in a million and one ways. This is of course only a result of our ingrained ignorance and folly, our lack of self-knowledge and honesty, and has precious little to do with authentic creativity.

It is also very important to understand that the lack of true meaning and purpose is a defining characteristic and inevitable consequence of the materialistic view of life currently embedded into our culture and civilisation, so it is hardly surprising that so many people experience life as being meaningless and without true purpose. After all, if there is no life after death and we are all going to die soon enough, what's the point of it all? If life is nothing but a haphazard and random series of intrinsically meaningless events, how can we ever hope to find meaning, purpose and truth at all? We can't of course, but that's the price we are forced to pay if we insist on embracing a materialistic and mechanistic view of life and all creation. We cannot expect to find meaning and purpose in a philosophy that effectively denies the boundless creativity, intelligence and compassion of life itself, and hence our lives often seem dull, empty, wasted and pointless.

The problems we typically find ourselves facing often have their roots in the unconscious and monumental fear of the abysmal void we occasionally may sense within ourselves. The deep-rooted fear of not existing as a clearly defined personality or ego frightens many of us from exploring the miracle of being and the mystery of consciousness. In itself, there is nothing wrong with the ego and the appearance of being somebody, but it is necessary all the same to transcend such limitations in order to start becoming aware of that which is the source of everything on the level of both inner and outer form. A sense of identity based on thought, mind-stuff and everything that has to do with me and mine, is ultimately an illusion, and even though we have to use words like me and mine for practical reasons, they certainly don't refer to anything that ultimately can be considered real.

If you want to know yourself as you truly are, you need to let go of everything you think you know and all preconceived ideas about yourself and life. If you happen to be a spiritual seeker, you may well have been hankering for truth, meaning, enlightenment and all the great, big swashbuckling answers for God knows how long, but being a seeker is no guarantee for winning the top prize in the spiritual sweepstakes. Most people of a spiritual or religious inclination are either permanently stuck in a rigid and often oppressive belief-system, or wandering ceaselessly from one teaching to another, one method to another, one guru to another, trying almost everything currently available in the spiritual marketplace in their search for salvation or enlightenment.

Moreover, on such a journey, it is not uncommon to pass through states of total meaninglessness and lack of interest in everything that you are usually busying yourself with. Sometimes it can seem as if nothing of what you have ever done, read, practised or been involved in has been of any real significance, and in a manner of speaking that might be closer to the truth than you think. It does have an indirect significance though, but the real issue here is that there is nothing you can do directly to bring about authentic realisation of your true nature. The reason for this isn't that the truth of what you are is far away, or otherwise unattainable. Quite the contrary, there is no distance at all between you and the truth of what you are. This is because you are already the truth, just the way you are. Any effort to reach it, to purify yourself, develop yourself or become enlightened is therefore ultimately doomed to fail precisely because all these activities tend to send you on a journey away from what you are, and won't help you realise that you already are what you are looking for.

I don't know if you have ever felt as if your life has turned into some kind of uncomfortable and ridiculous parody of a very bad theatre performance, but if you have ever experienced such a state, that is actually very good, and something to welcome with open arms. You may be familiar with the myth of Sisyphus, who was sentenced to roll a great big heavy rock up a steep hill, only to have it roll back down again, repeating this arduous task ad infinitum. If you ever feel as if you have been condemned to play a similar kind of role, that might not at first seem very uplifting, but nonetheless it is an experience that sooner or later, and with a bit of luck, everybody is likely to pass through in some form or another.

In spite of what popular opinion might have to say about such matters, it is by no means negative to experience everything as being meaningless, wasted and having the feeling that there is no way out. Quite the contrary, this feeling of total despair can be truly positive and conducive to the realisation of truth, because this kind of experience may well awaken a thirst and longing for truth that can ultimately be satisfied only by the full realisation of who you truly are. And if, on top of that, one can manage to live in that state of constructive despair without drawing conclusions about it, or wishing for things to be different than what they are, so much the better.

Everybody goes through difficult and challenging experiences and states during the journey of life, but sooner or later we will all come to realise that it is all good and often a kind of blessing in disguise. Life never does anything without good reason, and it is through our suffering and hard times that we are most likely to realise that none of it can ever touch us or change what we truly are. If you haven't already, you will eventually realise that what you are is universal consciousness itself, and as such you are immortal and indestructible. You will know that nothing that happens, no matter how painful or traumatic it might be, can ever hurt or stain you. Once you realise this, even death is a piece of cake and nothing to be worried about. When your number comes up and the time has come to lay down your mortal coil and bid this crazy, strange and beautiful world a final goodbye, it's something to be welcomed and celebrated.

The greatest gifts of life often come through hardship and suffering, and may indeed help you finally realise that you are one with all, that the wellspring of all is consciousness itself and that you are it. Then life becomes a benediction, and unconditional love may effortlessly flower.

There are simply no limits to how life can be experienced and what it can reveal to you. The moment you surrender and let yourself go, anything is possible. The only barriers you are likely to run up against are your own ideas of life, yourself and what is real. Life is an amazing adventure, a wondrous journey into the unknown. If you think you've got it all figured out and know all the answers, or if you happen to live through some form of mind-based kind of identity, you will never be able to penetrate beyond the most superficial layers of existence. A high degree of maturity as well as great courage and not the least inner strength are required to let go of the mainstream hallucinatory perception of reality and realise the truth of who you are.

I am not a spiritual teacher and have no desire to guide or advise anyone when it comes to spiritual matters, but if I were to give any kind of general advice at all, it would have to be to spend time with nature as often and as much as you can. If at all possible, seek out places where the incessant noise of the modern world is greatly diminished or preferably absent altogether. Breathe fresh air and feel your unbreakable connection with the beautiful Earth and all that grows from it. Tune in to what nature is silently telling you, and you will sooner or later realise that you are as vast and limitless as the sky itself. Layers upon layers of meaning and significance may then spontaneously be revealed to you.

When you merge with the beauty and perfection of nature, you are being blessed with ever deeper states of communion with existence. There are no limits to what nature and life itself can teach you, and whenever you are in nature, admiring and enjoying the sunshine, the rain, the snow, the wind, the trees, the flowers, the mountains, the rivers, the lakes, the ocean, the clouds, the stars, the sky and all the rest of it, you are nurtured at a much deeper level than you might be aware of. As you may or may not know, and whether you are in the right frame of mind to admit to it or not, you are always and forever one with the totality of life, currently expressing itself as your physical, mental and emotional appearance and the particular circumstances of your life.

And in case you are still pondering the meaning of life, and especially if you are looking for some kind of spiritual practice, a path to enlightenment or whatever else you might fancy along such lines, I have a very simple suggestion for you: Be kind. Just be kind and considerate to all living beings, to nature, to the environment and even to all man-made objects. The simple act of continuous and consistent kindness is a much more advanced, practical and powerful tool than even the most sophisticated meditations, intricate religious rituals and highfaluting spiritual practices. It is precisely this simple and gentle kindness to all life that will eventually transform the world. The consistent practice of selfless kindness and heartfelt generosity is ultimately what will bring about the dawn of a new humanity populating a new Earth.

The sanctity of life

Once you strip away the extraneous and sometimes confusing paraphernalia of philosophy, ideology and religion, the meaning of life and the truth of being are not complicated or difficult at all. What you are is not something mysterious and inaccessible that can only be experienced or realised through advanced meditations, complicated exercises, renunciation, austerities and suchlike. No, I would say it is something so simple and self-evident that most people tend to overlook it completely. You are nothing and everything, both at the same time. You are nothing in the sense that the ego that you think you are doesn't actually exist, and you are everything in the sense that your true nature is the oneness of consciousness that is all. It has been said that when you realise that you are nothing at all, that is wisdom, and when you realise that you are all and everything, that is love. I have no idea who first came up with that, but it's a pretty good way of putting it, regardless of its source.

There is no separation anywhere. That is an illusion that exists only within the human mind, a mind that habitually tends to divide everything up into ever smaller bits and pieces, and that loves to categorise, define and figure it all out in verbal and intellectual ways. All the compartmentalisation and fragmentation that the mind is capable of do of course have some practical value, but they tend to obscure the realisation of the true reality and oneness of all life. Everything that exists is a spontaneous expression of the infinite creativity of life itself. What you are is one with the creative intelligence that is universal consciousness, the one consciousness that is the source of all life and its many manifestations, with your body-mind form obviously being one of them.

Feel free to call this intelligence or ultimate reality God or whatever else that takes your fancy, because the name is of no importance at all. This creative, intelligent consciousness is not only the essence of everything, but also that which everything is made from. Another way of putting it is to say that it flows through all forms of life, is the source of all phenomena, that everything appears within it and that it appears as everything. While being everything we can ever sense, know and experience, it is simultaneously far beyond all of it. Its innumerable modes of expression are in a state of continuous flux, and its unlimited creative power is always overflowing with abundance, vitality and freshness. This is a totally spontaneous process and is the wellspring of all our creative endeavours. We are all actively involved in this creative outpouring, while also being one of its expressions. We are the eternal divine joyously playing with itself.

So what is the purpose of all this, where does it all come from and what is its ultimate meaning? There might not even be an answer to those kind of questions, but in any case, I would suggest that you put your most sceptical hat on straight away if anyone, including me, ever starts dishing out explanations as to where, why, what, how and so on. We can only ever speculate, and that is precisely what we've been busying ourselves with throughout the ages.

For as long as humans have existed, scholars, pundits, philosophers, sages and other more or less self-styled experts have been pondering what the meaning of life is, why we are here, where we might be heading after death and so on. Such speculation naturally only tends to create more confusion, because consciousness in the sense of the infinitely creative intelligence of being is the only phenomenon that is real in the absolute sense, even though strictly speaking it is not a phenomenon at all.

The human mind can never grasp what the creative intelligence of universal consciousness really is, because it is something that just can't be understood or explained intellectually. It is much too big for that or rather it's totally beyond size, shape and other measurable quantities. The emptiness that is the ultimate fullness can never be explained on the level of mind, and neither can it be found through the senses, at least not directly. It is real for you only to the extent that you have seen through and discarded any idea of yourself as a separate individual so that you no longer identify yourself with anything in particular. Then you will know the truth, but you won't necessarily be able to say anything about it, because there might not be anything that can be said. This all-inclusive creative consciousness is infinite, eternal intelligence of a totally different magnitude and quality to anything that we can ever relate to as human beings. It is just completely beyond anything we will ever be able to understand.

Let's look at it in a slightly different way by asking a very specific question: "What is God?" In the conventional sense of the word, it is nothing but an idea or a belief, which is totally void of any kind of substance, sense, meaning or reality. God as the old man in the sky kind of chap who created everything and will punish anyone who disobeys him with eternal torture of the most excruciating kind must surely be one of the most absurd ideas the human mind has ever come up with. It is claimed that God created man in his own image, but that is of course sheer balderdash. The God that the priestly representatives of various religions have always been trying to brainwash us into believing in can more accurately be described as man's own creation. That God is nothing more than an invention of the human mind, and yet the fundamental message of the priesthood seems to be that we must strive to make this God happy so that *he* can make *us* happy. Does that kind of reasoning seem reasonable or intelligent to you? Well, I don't know about you, but that kind of reasoning just sounds like codswallop to me.

Instead of God creating us in his image, isn't it obvious that we have literally created God in our own image, more or less as a glorified version of ourselves? It is universally prevalent to see God as a personal force or some kind of superman who has created the universe and who has total, unlimited power over all and everything. Christianity, for example, would have us believe that God is sitting up there in a non-specified location known as Heaven, watching our every move, while considering whether we should be rewarded or punished. The only problem with this scenario of course is that there is no such thing as God as a person. Such primitive ideas probably have their roots in man's urge to have someone to depend on and turn to for answers. The image of God as almighty heavenly Father is well and truly obsolete and ought to have been discarded by now, but all the same it is obvious that it is still a vital part of most people's psyche, regardless of whether their beliefs are of a religious or a materialist and atheist nature.

God isn't something that can be made into an object of belief, quite simply because God cannot be objectified, defined, described, categorised or otherwise labelled or put into any specific context. You might think that this is going way too far, but I would say that to believe in God is somewhat absurd, although not nearly as absurd as believing in atheism and materialism. The religious kind of belief in God can even be viewed as a kind of sophisticated form of blasphemy. Yes, I do think it can be described as blasphemy because belief is always within the limits of what can be defined or objectified, and God is far beyond anything like that. A traditional belief in God essentially amounts to denying the omniscient and omnipresent reality of God and our own intrinsic oneness with all that is.

If we are to use the word God in any meaningful way at all, it can only be as another word for the totality of all that is. It is the creative, intelligent, consciousness that is everything yet also beyond everything; it is the ultimate source of all. All forms of life are unique expressions of the divine, which is conscious, creative intelligence of a magnitude and power that we can't ever hope to understand. But still, we can be one with it, quite simply because that is ultimately what we are. God is another name for life itself, for the totality that is all and everything.

Another way of putting it is to say that God is what you are, but even though that is true it is important to realise that you are not God. Do you see the difference? If you say, "I am God," it implies that you are God as opposed to everybody else who is something else, but that is clearly absurd. But if you realise that what you are as universal consciousness is what God is, then you will have risen above the common misunderstanding that we are separate entities living in an objectively real world. You will know that all is one. What you are is the very essence of life and divinity no matter what you do or what happens to you, and irrespective of what others might tell you to the contrary. It is only a question of waking up to the truth of what you are, and that requires no time or effort at all. It is a spontaneous flowering that is uncaused and it will always remain a glorious and inexplicable mystery.

Anyone who thinks that they are somebody, a separate entity, will necessarily also think of God as a separate being, regardless of whether they believe in such an almighty chap or not. In your essence, you are not somebody; you are nobody, quite literally nobody, and so is everybody else. Realising this is inevitable in the long run, because you cannot forever avoid seeing the most obvious and simple thing ever. And don't even think about doing something to get this understanding. There isn't really anything to get, and as if that wasn't enough, neither is there is anywhere to go, nobody who could go there and nothing to achieve anyway. In fact, whatever you might try to do to reach the truth can only take you away from it, quite simply because you are it. The realisation of all this is something that happens in spite of all your efforts, not because of them. The vast creative power that is the totality of life itself awakens this understanding within you. The all-embracing consciousness that is all awakens to its own reality through you. This intelligence is the infinite, eternal being that is all and everything, the divinity that is life itself, and you are that.

Religion

The human mind is the consummate and undisputed world champion of division, duality and separation. For God knows how many thousands of years, we have been trying to understand life, the universe and everything by splitting it all up into ever smaller parts, which are then studied and categorised for future reference. This process has made us increasingly incapable of seeing the bigger picture and the wholeness and oneness of all life. The materialist culture that is currently predominant on this planet is so deep-rooted within the psyche of the vast majority of people that most of us never even question this outdated and fragmentary worldview. Seeing yourself as a separate entity living in an objectively real material world that exists independently of consciousness has become the default mental and ideological setting for nearly all of us.

An inevitable part of this worldview, with all its compartmentalisation and fragmentation, is the artificial split of life into matter and spirit. This way of seeing things has been adopted not only by diehard materialists, but also by those who call themselves religious. Virtually all religious people, regardless of which religion they adhere to and which God they happen to worship, are convinced that they are separate entities that live in a material world that exists independently of themselves. Even though they may believe in a God and an afterlife, in a sense that is still nothing more than a cleverly dressed-up version of materialism, because religious people's idea of heaven is still a world existing outside of themselves, one that they may or may not be granted access to after death. And if they're not allowed into the heavenly realms with all its many pleasures, the agonies of hell are waiting. It's all totally illogical, irrational and preposterous of course, but the point is that the religious teachings about an afterlife of heaven, hell or whatever else are all pure duality, which necessarily is also a denial of the oneness of all life.

Matter and spirit don't have any real existence as opposing or even complementary forces or phenomena. The meaningless divisions into body and soul, spiritual and material, sacred and profane, good and evil, God and devil, are all the inevitable expressions of the hard-core dualism that is the abiding curse of the human mind. This dualism is a direct result of nearly everybody's fundamental belief in being a separate entity living in an objectively real world and is the root cause of all the conflicts, misery and suffering of this world. This way of interpreting life has been automatically inherited down through untold generations and is the true meaning of the term original sin used in Christian theology.

According to Biblical lore, Adam and Eve were unfortunate enough to help themselves to the fruits from the tree of knowledge about good and evil, after which nothing could ever be the same again. This is of course an allegory, a symbolic tale, but it's a beautiful and elegantly told story that explains in simple terms how we came to create and manifest such an incredibly complex and conflict-ridden reality for ourselves. Once you start to split everything up into categories of good and evil, negative and positive, sacred and profane and so on, you are perpetuating the original sin, which is nothing more than the split between the me on the inside, and the other or world on the outside. In other words, it is the bog standard materialist worldview of separate entities living in an objectively real material world that exists independently of consciousness.

The teachings contained in the Bible and other religious texts are often very perceptive, and a lot of truth can be found in them, but only if you know how to read them. That can be difficult without a clear understanding of your true nature, but at the same time it is relatively easy for anyone with a minimum of intelligence and an open mind to sense that there is at least some truth in many religious teachings.

This has been cleverly exploited by the priesthood of various religions for many centuries. They have always been very creative in finding ways of conditioning people to follow their suggestions and thus create followers who are easy to control, instead of teaching people to think for themselves and find their own unique way to an authentic understanding of life, reality and their true nature.

A good example of how religious scriptures and teachings have been used to confuse and mislead people down the ages is the tendency for religious preachers to teach suppression of the body's natural needs. They have presented exalted ideals of salvation through renunciation and spiritual purity, but such a polarisation is bound to lead to inner conflict and suffering. It is bad enough that the division into spirit and matter is rather meaningless, but what is worse is that many of the ideals and goals of the religions are nothing more than psychological straightjackets. If we are to understand and value life totally, we have to realise that it is a living and creative process of wholeness that can never truly be split into different parts. Consciousness, mind, energy, spirit and matter are all one in the sense that all forms of life in every dimension and realm are fundamentally just modulations of consciousness, and unique expressions of the power that is all and everything.

The only reality is consciousness itself, but all the same we do have to relate to what we think of as matter and physical phenomena in daily life as if they are objectively real. We just can't get around that, no matter how hard we try, but that is all part of the weird and wonderful mystery of life and does not have to be a problem for anyone. There is nothing wrong with talking about matter and physical reality as far as the practical details of life are concerned, but strictly speaking, it is not relevant to this discussion. And by the way, has anyone ever actually been able to fully understand or explain what matter and physical phenomena such as gravity, mass, electricity and magnetism really are? The clever clogs of science might claim to be able to understand and explain it all, but have any of their many explanations and elucidations ever made much difference? No, I don't think so either.

If we are to be honest with ourselves, we don't really know anything, we only think we do. This so-called physical reality is a very mysterious and strange place indeed, in fact it is so utterly and phenomenally weird that we can't even begin to imagine how outrageously outlandish it truly is. It is like a very sophisticated and enigmatic riddle that the human mind can never fully solve. Instead of accepting and living with our ignorance, we seem to find it much easier to think that we know a whole lot of really clever stuff, and we love nothing more than deceiving ourselves into thinking that we are the most advanced and sophisticated civilisation ever to have existed on the face of the Earth. This is of course an illusion, and the proof that we are still a rather primitive and underachieving civilisation is the absolute mess we have made of life on Earth. We are systematically abusing and destroying the natural world, as well as constantly trying to find ever more efficient ways of killing each other. What in Heaven's name is so clever and advanced about any of that?

And yet, in spite of our monumental ignorance, monstrous urge for destruction, self-satisfied arrogance and blatant stupidity, we seem to think that we know for a fact that there really is something like an independently existing world of material objects. We take the material world for granted without ever questioning it, and many of our most eminent scientists are keeping themselves busy by searching for the key to its enigma by splitting everything into smaller and smaller pieces.

A classic and fairly recent example of this is the construction of the so-called Large Hadron Collider, which by an astronomically wide margin surely must be the largest and most expensive toy the world has ever seen. It is ostensibly supposed to help physicists find answers to the most fundamental questions in their area of expertise, and I can only wish them the best of luck with that endeavour. To be honest, they might as well ask the cat for those answers, because the more answers they think they have found, the more questions will arise from those answers, and none of it will ever help us live in harmony and peace with each other, quite the contrary. Apparently, one of the success stories so far of this gigantic monstrosity of knick-knack is finding some kind of subatomic particle they call the Higgs boson, although what they think they're going to use that for is anybody's guess. The underlying assumption to this kind of highfaluting nonsense, as well as a whole lot of other mind games currently passed off as science, is that matter is not only real and the basis on which everything else exists, but that there is an objective reality out there at all. This is indeed the paradigm presently accepted as ultimate truth, yet it is all built on illogical theories and unproven assumptions, and on closer scrutiny none of them have any validity beyond purely practical purposes.

In any case, science itself has indisputably shown us that matter is mostly empty space, so even from a strictly scientific point of view, thinking that anything like solid objects exists is a fallacy. It is probably closer to the truth to say that it is all energy, but even that is just a word that in the long run doesn't really explain much at all. Science may have managed to make some headway towards understanding how the various constituents of what we call matter behave and how they relate to each other, but as long as our outlook on life is predominantly rational, reductionist, intellectual and materialistic, we will remain stuck in the dark ages with no chance of ever penetrating the mysteries of nature and life. What we think of as physical reality exists only as an expression of the one consciousness or being that is the true source and ultimate reality of everything. That source is the essence of who you are and what life is.

If you want to know what life is, you can't automatically accept that the physical world exists as an independent reality, and that it is anything at all like what you perceive it to be. You can never see reality as it is by help of your senses only anyway. It is always going to be a purely subjective experience, and a material world independent of consciousness quite simply doesn't exist in the terms we usually think of it. The physical world that we seem to inhabit is real only in the sense that it is a modulation of universal consciousness. To put it into somewhat more poetic language, the world of objects and phenomena is an endlessly fascinating and utterly beguiling fantasy in God's infinite mind, so in that sense it is real. It is common in this connection to raise the objection that extreme pleasure or pain is irrefutable proof that what we perceive through our senses must be real, but this argument is totally illogical. Even the most excruciating pain and the most heavenly pleasure can never prove anything at all about reality, for the intensity of the painful or pleasurable sense impressions may well also be illusory.

This is all fair enough, but what does it matter? What difference does it really make whether we think the physical world is real or an illusion? That is a valid point, and in actual fact it doesn't make much difference at all what we think about any of this. It amounts to the same whether we say that everything is real or an illusion, matter or spirit, because none of these words can do anything to destroy the invisible cobweb of dualism and ignorance we have entangled ourselves in. It is highly doubtful that the human mind will ever be capable of understanding the true nature of life, and it may not even be meant to grasp it, but when the all-embracing presence that exists beyond all duality wakes up from the dream of mind, thought, separation and ego, everything becomes clear. That doesn't mean that life can be explained or categorised on ar intellectual level, or that it is possible to put the truth of life into words at all, but there's no need for that anyway. It's only the egocentric human mind that seeks explanations and formulas to categorise life. Consciousness, which is what we are and what everything is, is beyond categorisation and explanation, and can't be put into a formula.

Scientists give the appearance of having made great strides in understanding what life is and how the universe seems to work, but unless they turn their attention inwards to explore the truth of what they are, they will never be able to fully understand life. As long as they accept the assumptions that the prevailing world culture of materialism is built on and which are hardly ever questioned, it's all going to remain an impenetrable mystery. Until humanity turns its attention toward that which is aware of it all, even the brightest and most highly educated of us will continue to fumble around in darkness and ignorance, without hope of ever stumbling upon any other meaning to life than what their conditioned minds can fantasise and dream about.

It is fairly uncommon that anyone voluntarily abandons the dualistic and fragmentary way of relating to life that has become so common that it is regarded as normal. We have all been brainwashed into accepting a worldview that is built on separation, ego and materialistic values. Until we break free from this invisible prison we are bound to continue our painful journey down endless thorny avenues of duality and conflict. The path of freedom and harmony is always available, but very few people seem to be interested or willing to embark on a journey along the road less travelled and thus be courageous enough to take the plunge into the unknown.

There is no other real freedom than freedom from the known, and as the great spiritual teacher J. Krishnamurti once famously said: *"Truth is a pathless land, and you cannot approach it by any path whatsoever, by any religion, by any sect [...] Truth, being limitless, unconditioned, unapproachable by any path whatsoever, cannot be organized; nor should any organization be formed to lead or coerce people along a particular path."* Those are indeed words of great wisdom and understanding.

Life is a dynamic process of incessant creativity, movement, change and evolution held in the formless embrace of universal consciousness. Life is an inscrutable miracle, and a marvellous manifestation of an intelligence far beyond what we can ever understand or explain. A religious life in the true meaning of the word is one that is lived in devotion to life itself, and that sees everything as a manifestation of the divine.

The religions that have developed over the centuries may well be paths that many people still need to travel, but whether those paths are labelled Christianity, Buddhism, Judaism, Islam, Hinduism or anything else, they tend to be built on dogmas, rituals and traditions that are of little or no value in the quest for ultimate truth. It might have been a necessity for the human race to go down this road, but isn't it time we realised that in terms of truth realisation and the manifestation of peace on Earth it is a road that leads nowhere?

Moreover, what is generally known as the life of the spirit is often such a thoroughly dull and lifeless affair that you could almost suspect the devil himself to be in charge of it. The long-faced seriousness of the average religious person is really nothing but a sophisticated form of blasphemy, whereas a sense of humour is often the most appropriate response to the many ups and downs of life.

But unfortunately, religion is for the most part a very serious business, and most religions demand, either implicitly or explicitly, that you should follow their teachings without question, and that the only way to salvation is to be found through their specific system and nowhere else. Priests. bishops, popes, imams, swamis, lamas, rabbis, or whatever else they might be called, have taken on the role as the indispensable connection between humanity and God, but in actual fact most of them often function as an awkward and nearly impenetrable barrier to the realisation of truth.

On the one hand the priests entice us with promises of eternal salvation and their own particular version of heaven, though only if you subscribe to their teaching with all its absurd directives. And if you don't stick to the only way, they threaten you with agonising suffering in blackest hell for all eternity, or whatever else they can come up with within the realms of morbid and beastly punishment. All this does is fan the flames of greed and fear, which have been the curse of humanity for millennia. Most people are hardly even aware of this, because living one's life in fear and greed has become so universally prevalent that it is considered perfectly normal.

It is true that at least in the Western world the position and power of the traditional religions have gradually become considerably diminished over the last century or so, but the internal and external chaos that has been created throughout history by religious doctrine and practice is nevertheless still in full bloom.

After all, isn't the way religion manifests and operates in the world just an indication of what kind of developmental level our civilisation is operating from? It seems to me that contemporary religion is a perfect expression of where we're at in spiritual terms. Most of us obviously have a desperate need to have something to believe in and something to hope for. It is a widespread notion that it is important or even essential to have something to believe in, but very few believers seem to have discovered that belief always begets violence and conflict.

Beliefs not only function as a kind of substitute for true knowledge, but also tend to lead to conflict and violence. Our inner divisions make humanity split into national, political, ethnic and religious groups that as a matter of course fall out with each other more often than not. As long as people insist on believing in something, and insist on being Christians,

Muslims, Hindus, Buddhists, Communists, or atheists for that matter, they are also bound to be at odds with each other. This is as certain as hallelujah and amen in church and moreover so self-evident that it shouldn't be necessary to mention it at all. It is also obvious that our need for living in the false hope of a better future or even for eternal salvation makes us unable to be one with the plain and simple reality of life as it continuously reveals itself right now. With all its beliefs, dogmas and promises of salvation, religion is really nothing more than a relatively sophisticated version of our relentless urge to escape from ourselves.

The tragic truth is that virtually all religions and sects, whether they are big or small, function as a kind of metaphysical intoxicant for their adherents. Organised religion more often than not is like a pacifier for those who have neither the courage nor inclination to explore the deeper truth of life. It is true that all religions have a grain of truth in them, even if it is usually well hidden beneath all sorts of theatrical shenanigans and pretentious mumbo-jumbo. Most of us can intuitively sense that something authentic could possibly be hiding in there somewhere, but the majority of people seem unable to distinguish the wheat from the chaff, and therefore take potluck and accept stones for bread.

Why do so many of us need to have some kind of belief to cling to in the first place? Isn't it because we don't know ourselves and what life is? Belief just means that we are not interested in the truth, or in what is ultimately real. You don't have to believe in what you know and understand. Whoever is attuned to the flow of life has no need for believing in anything.

When you know what you are, there is no longer any room for belief, speculation and second-hand opinions, because they are all nothing but substitutes for truth. Knowing yourself as consciousness is enough on to itself, and once that knowledge has manifested in you, no further seeking is necessary or even possible, because you will know that there is nothing of lasting value to achieve beyond knowing what you are. All other kinds of human achievements pale by comparison to knowing yourself, because they are ultimately all temporary, whereas true self-knowledge is eternal. A natural life lived in freedom from the known is uncluttered by belief, and is a religious life in the best and most authentic sense of the word. To put it simply, life itself is the only true religion, nature is its only temple and loving kindness is its only spiritual practice.

Meditation

Most people who can be bothered to have an opinion about it believe that inner development and spiritual progress can best be advanced by means of prayer, meditation or some kind of concentrated mental effort, and that a spiritual practice along such lines is the quickest way to enlightenment. There are millions of people all over the world who put a great deal of time and effort into practising some kind of method or technique to reach enlightenment, nirvana, happiness, truth, various heavenly spheres or whatever other rewards they envision for themselves. However, when it comes to realising the plain and simple truth of who you are and of what life is, all methods, systems and techniques are distractions more than anything else. Self-realisation isn't really a question of effort, but rather of direct insight, a spontaneous knowing of the essence of what you are.

There is of course absolutely nothing wrong with practising meditation and other spiritual disciplines, in fact it can be very beneficial, and I for one am all for it. I am convinced that if more people set aside time for meditation and other spiritual practices regularly, the world would be a much better place in all respects. The point I'm trying to make is that even though there are many different forms of meditation which can affect both mind and body quite powerfully and positively, there is no method that can lead you to the truth of who you are, quite simply because you are already this truth, just the way you are right now. A method or technique is nothing but yet another activity, which will usually have an effect and some relevance in the world of form, space and time, but what you are is beyond all that.

Spiritual transformation is the realisation of that which is beyond form, space and time, and it is not related to any activity you can ever engage in, no matter how advanced it may be. Whatever methods and techniques you might feel drawn to more often than not tend to be practised with an eye to results, in the hope of achieving something in an imaginary future. The spiritual practitioner surely wants to achieve something or other regardless of what method he or she is using, and this desire can act as a barrier to perceiving the truth of what you are. A wish or a desire always finds a way of projecting itself into a fictitious future, while freedom and truth only exist in the eternal now, in the full realisation of what you truly are.

A different way of relating to meditation is to see it as what you are, not something that you do. Following on from this you could say that the separate and ultimately non-existent self is an activity or a process, and not what we are. Usually we tend to see the separate self as what we are and meditation as something that this egocentric self does from time to time, but if you look at it from this different perspective, your approach to meditation will start to change. Meditation in this sense is beyond method, beyond anything that the mind can do or even think about. It is a way of life that embraces the totality of one's whole existence, because it is ultimately what you are, which is consciousness itself. In this sense, meditation means the absence of the meditator, and the absence of anything that is meditated upon.

You could also say that meditation is a quality of consciousness; a spontaneous blossoming which happens independently of the mind's incessant activity and irrelevant interference. Meditation in this sense of the word isn't really something that can be practised or in any way be forced into being. Nobody can do anything directly to bring this about, and contrary to what many people so stubbornly assert, there is nobody, neither in Heaven nor on Earth, who can give you this gift. Nobody can give you what you already are.

Meditation is usually thought of as practising some kind of

method or technique, with an eye to reach a predefined goal, however vague that goal might be. I would like to suggest that the word meditation in its most fundamental sense means awareness and conscious oneness with universal being.

There are of course innumerable methods of meditation, each with their own benefits and virtues, and while most methods are valuable enough, they do not in and by themselves cause spiritual maturity or awakening. Meditation in the sense of practising a method tends to nurture the illusion of a separate entity doing something to achieve some kind of goal. Once you move beyond such narrow confinements, you start exploring the effortless lightness of pure being, beyond dualities, form and action. It is this realm of grace that is the wellspring of peace, harmony and goodness. If we look at it this way, it's obvious that meditation isn't really something you can do or take ownership of in any way. At the most the only practice you can engage in is to be open to the unknown, resting in the knowing of yourself as limitless awareness alone.

You might still be wondering if there is a place for some kind of meditative practice to help you reach that state of peace and harmony that we all intuitively long for. If what you want is to reach a state of mind that is relatively peaceful, harmonious and still, there are certainly many methods of meditation that can be of help to you. That is all very valuable and commendable, but that isn't really what I am talking about. The realisation of the truth of yourself as universal consciousness has nothing to do with states of peace and stillness, although there is good reason to claim that peace and stillness are more likely to manifest themselves through someone who knows him- or herself as consciousness. In other words, there isn't anything you can do or practise to realise the deepest truth of who you are. You are already that truth. You just need to stop and see that what you are looking for is what is looking. It is neither difficult nor easy because it doesn't rely on or refer to anything that you can do.

However, if you believe that it is necessary for you to do something to realise the truth, then you might as well get on with it, regardless of what it is, if not for anything else than to transcend the illusion that there is a method that can be used to get you there. At the most you could say that whatever you do or whatever happens to you is a necessary step in your journey of awakening, but it is important to realise that there isn't anything that in and of itself is an absolute requirement for awakening to the truth of who you are. It is a widespread notion that you have to purify, perfect or develop yourself in some way to realise truth, but that is a fallacy, because you are already the truth, just the way you are now. Nothing needs to be added. On your journey through life with all its ups and downs, you may well have to do a lot to achieve certain goals, but in the context of self-realisation, all that is needed is quite simply to let go of the illusion that you are a particular somebody who needs to do something or other in order to achieve anything at all.

But maybe you're still wondering if there is any virtue in trying to still the mind and go beyond thinking. Who knows, there might well be, and if you feel drawn to this kind of endeavour, just go for it, but please do bear in mind that thinking itself is not the problem. Mental silence and ignorance can quite easily coexist, so having a still mind is neither a prerequisite nor a help in realising the truth of who you are. Thinking is a completely natural and spontaneous process, and it becomes problematic only when identification with it arises.

If thought thinks that there is an entity like a thinker who is thinking thoughts and that this thinker needs to stop thinking so that it can achieve something, become enlightened or whatever, then you have set yourself up for conflict and ultimate defeat. Trying to stop thinking is a battle you can't win, because doing that is nothing but thought trying to stop itself. It is as futile as trying to pull yourself up by your own shoestrings. It is not going to work. Many people of a spiritual inclination think that they should not be thinking, but this is just thought fighting with itself. Even worse off are those who are delusional enough to think that they are not thinking. Believe it or not, but I have actually come across a few of those as well.

All this struggle to stop thinking is more often than not a waste of time and energy. Once you have realised that you are not the thinker, that there is in fact no thinker, only thoughts, then this question will no longer arise. Thinking just happens, doesn't it? There is nobody there who thinks or does anything. There is no thinker and thinking is something that happens quite spontaneously. You don't have to waste time and energy trying to fight it, because that is nothing more than the mind wrestling with itself.

Thought in itself isn't the problem Thinking is a natural activity and becomes problematic only when thought starts saying: "I don't want this – I want that!" The thought of "I" may be a practical necessity, but when taken to be a distinct, separate entity it is bound to create conflict and suffering. There is no thinker separate from thought and no I within as a distinct and isolated entity. Our true identity is not to be found in thought or any other temporary phenomenon. Only awareness itself is forever the same and always present. Therefore it is not strictly speaking true to say, "I am aware," because there is no I separate from awareness. A statement that would be more in line with truth is this: "I am awareness." You don't have awareness; awareness is what you are. There is no separate self that has awareness. Only awareness is aware.

Awareness or consciousness is unlimited and eternal. This is everybody's experience, and strictly speaking, all anyone ever experiences is consciousness, because that's all that there ever is. Nobody has ever found a limit or border to consciousness, because it isn't a definable object. Consciousness is the formless, yet all forms are contained within it. Everything you sense, perceive or experience is literally made from consciousness, and nothing has any separate kind of existence apart from consciousness. So there are not two things: manifestation and consciousness. All is consciousness, yet consciousness being the formless, infinite and eternal unborn depends on nothing. It simply is what it is. It is the ultimate reality and it is what we are. Take your stand as awareness and welcome all of life as it is with love and acceptance.

In spite of the fact that thought isn't actually an obstacle for spiritual awakening, it is hard to deny that in most spiritual circles thought has nearly always been seen as the bad guy, nothing short of the ultimate villain, and a lot of spiritual practice tends to be centred on getting rid of thought. Once upon a time I happened to come across an audio program called "How to stop thinking", and while it was well put together and quite interesting, it was also obvious that every single word in that presentation was a thought, and that presenting a program like that relies completely on thought and some kind of mental activity to make any sense at all. You don't need to get rid of thoughts. You just need to understand that you are not the thinker, that there isn't a thinker as such and that thought is a completely spontaneous and natural process that presents absolutely no obstacle to the realisation of your true nature.

You may well be thinking that if you are not the one who is thinking thoughts or doing things, if there truly is nobody there, then who is it that is thinking or doing stuff? The answer to that question is quite simply that nobody is ever thinking or doing anything. Everything just happens as a spontaneous outpouring of life itself. You are the all-embracing and eternal presence of pure being in which thoughts, feelings and actions naturally come and go.

A good metaphor for this is the infinity of the sky above us. Imagine looking at the beautiful blue sky on a lovely summer's day, or better still, if you're reading this on a sunny day, just go to a quiet and beautiful place in nature and spend some time looking at the sky. Just relax into it and let it embrace you. If you do, you may well realise that it can be seen as a perfect outer representation of what you are, of your essential being. When you look up at the blue sky, you are essentially looking at nothing. You are looking at infinity, the unfathomable vastness of deep space. That is the most accurate manifestation on the outer level of what you are, as if the emptiness of the clear blue sky is your formless being, somehow externalised. If there are some clouds drifting across this endless depth of nothingness we see as the blue sky, we can stretch the metaphor even further and see the clouds as representing your thoughts and feelings, or even as whatever happens to you in life. It is obvious that the emptiness of the blue sky is not in any way affected by the clouds drifting by. All the clouds come and go, yet the all-embracing presence of sky or deep space remains completely untouched by it all. In the same way, thoughts, emotions, actions and all the rest of it appear and disappear in the endless expanse of your true being.

If you let go of your urge to escape from the truth of what you are, and the erroneous notion that doing this, that or the other will award you something in the future, you may discover that mental activity starts to decrease of its own accord. You don't have to do anything, in fact the more you do the less successful you are going to be. You are already here now, so nothing else needs to happen or be done, other than letting go of any false ideas about who you are. Whenever you ask how, you are heading towards a dead end, because there are no answers on the level of the mind when it comes to realising the truth of who you are.

There is a lot of talk nowadays of living in the now and being present and so on, but it seems to me that for a lot of people that is just yet another way of trying to achieve a particular outcome and to reach some kind of desired state. Many spiritual seekers are putting a lot of time, effort and money into achieving more and better spiritual experiences and hopefully making them permanent, probably because they think that this will make them feel happy, peaceful and enlightened. Ultimately, however, this is never going to work, because regardless of what kind of experiences you have or what blissful states you reach, it will all fade away, and that's as certain as death itself, because any experience or state is nothing but yet another form that ultimately must disappear.

And whatever reasons people might have for wanting to get rid of thinking, none of it will ever deliver the goods. That's just something that's been accepted on hearsay. If you think it through properly, you will sooner or later realise that states and experiences come and go, and only the consciousness that you are forever remains. Consciousness is neither a state nor an experience, is never born, never dies, and cannot be defined, described or quantified in any way whatsoever. It is the omnipresent, omnipotent, omniscient reality of all that is.

As far as living in the now is concerned, isn't it obvious that the only reality you can ever know is life as it is now? But if you think you are elsewhere than here and now, and that reaching the now is going to bring some kind of benefit, you have already missed the only moment that ever exists, namely this one. As long as you think you are not in the present, staying in the now is going to remain an elusive goal, nothing but a pipe dream. You are of course always and eternally in the now, but if you think it should be different from what it is, you have a problem, so you need to find some formula for reaching and staying in the now, and on and on it goes.

Being present in this moment is completely natural and effortless, hence no techniques are necessary. Being present in the moment is not something that you can do or practise, because all doing in this respect is undertaken with a view to a future state of success. You are projecting yourself into an imagined future, even if you are doing that now. It doesn't matter what kind of tricks and techniques you try; trying to conquer your mind is a battle you are destined to lose. It's just thought fighting with itself, forever adding fuel to the fire of conflict.

Whatever practices and efforts you engage in, they will tend to reinforce the idea of a separate entity doing something in order to achieve some imagined fulfilment in a hypothetical future. There is nothing wrong with practising mindfulness and presence through whatever methods that may appeal to you, but if you think that you are a certain somebody who can do something, such as being aware and present in the moment, then you are really just running around in circles. Regardless of what techniques you use to still the mind and live in the moment, it is an approach that is never going to deliver the goods, because it just doesn't tackle the essential issue.

So what exactly is the essential issue? Nothing more nor less than realising the truth of who or what you are. Who is it that wants to stay in the now? Who is it that wants to go beyond thinking? Who is it that wants to become enlightened? Focus your attention on that, and all will be clear. But if you are still looking for something to practise or meditate upon, heed the wise words of the great spiritual teacher Jean Klein, who provided the following advice: *"Meditate on that which never changes."*

The crux of the matter is that before anything else, you need to find the truth of who you are. The question of identity needs to be tackled first. As far as truth realisation is concerned, practising a method or some kind of spiritual discipline tends to reinforce the idea of a separate entity trying to achieve something. If you are doing anything along spiritual lines with an eye to results, you are essentially just marching on the spot. You may have all sorts of great and mystical experiences, which may be valuable, fascinating, exciting and inspiring, but in terms of knowing what you are, experiences in themselves cannot provide the answer, because they are all temporary. What you are is eternal, beyond anything that happens or exists on the level of form, space and time.

Now is all there ever is and we can never ever be anywhere or anytime else than here and now. Living in the present moment can't be a goal, because you are already here and now anyway. A goal is necessarily separate from where and what you are here and now. It is a mental projection and can only take you further away from your natural state, which is conscious oneness with universal being. Once you have seen through all illusions and realised the truth of who you are, there is no question anymore of trying to live in the moment, because it is just so totally obvious to you that there is no other option anyway.

And in case you're wondering, let me just add that psychic abilities and mystical powers won't help you much either, so if what you are really interested in is the truth of what you are, you might as well forget about developing such powers. There are plenty of people who are very interested in these things, either by believing that psychic phenomena are real or believing that they are not. Because consciousness is the ultimate ground of all being and the true source of all appearances, there is really no question that all these things are more than possible, in fact they are constantly happening, but they are by no means more important than anything else. It is all whatever it is, as is everything else.

It is important to realise that such powers more often than not tend to act as an obstacle to realising the truth of what you are, quite simply because they can be so alluring. Occult faculties and esoteric knowledge may all be very exciting, but none of that stuff has ever helped anyone to realise the truth, no matter how fascinating it may all be. Psychic powers and experiences are not necessary for spiritual transformation, and they are certainly no indication that somebody is spiritually awake. There are quite a few people who are richly endowed with psychic abilities and know virtually everything about occult disciplines and the paranormal, but none of it really matters that much for somebody whose passion is self-knowledge and spiritual awakening. For the most part, people with psychic powers live in the same old way as everybody else, and they tend to have precisely the same prejudices and personal problems as anyone else.

It is only when you know yourself as universal consciousness, when you realise that you are one with all life, when you love unconditionally and thus live in harmony with all, that you will have found the only thing that is of lasting value. Then you will need neither esoteric knowledge nor psychic powers, in fact you won't need anything at all, because it's all nothing but a more or less interesting sideshow. What you are is enough, because what you are is all-inclusive, limitless and indestructible, and as such it is the only true reality.

When you know who you are you no longer attach any particular importance to the many forms that life takes. Instead you become more and more attuned to the essence of life itself, and so you are no longer distracted by psychic powers, spiritual experiences and suchlike. You may of course still be interested in these things, but the crucial difference is that you no longer feel reliant on anything in particular to make you happy and fulfilled. You abide as awareness and that is its own fulfilment. Life becomes a lot less complicated and the quiet contentment of simply being what you are is enough on to itself.

Eternity now, infinity here

Due to our cultural conditioning, we tend to think of eternity as endless time stretching from a distant past into an everlasting future. The notion that life perpetually moves from the past through the present into the future is quite a powerful one, but that notion is really just an alluring illusion the mind loves to lose itself in. We love the idea of development over time, because this gives us the chance to hope for a better future. We like to think that eternity consists of an infinite number of moments neatly arranged one after the other like pearls on a string, but this is a fallacy. There is only the now of eternal presence, and it embraces absolutely everything that exists. Eternity is now. Everything is created, maintained and destroyed in the presence of now, which is all there ever is.

Just as eternity has nothing to do with chronological time forever stretching away into the far-off distance of an imaginary future, infinity has nothing to do with endless space. There is only the infinity of what is, and if you are present to what is, you will notice that it is always here, fresh and vital. So our notions of time and space are really just the human mind's feeble interpretations of the infinity and eternity that is life here and now.

Neither time nor space as we usually think of them have any kind of objective existence apart from the purely functional and practical, yet it is far from easy to define space and time accurately. That's all right though, because after all they're just concepts. Very useful concepts for practical purposes, but without real existence, like a pale reflection of something real, and the illusion of their appearance must continually be created and maintained in order to retain its power.

Scientists are often trying to understand and explain time and space from a materialistic and mechanical perspective of reality, but that is an exercise in futility, or you could even say it's a waste of time. It's based on the unquestioned assumption that the foundation for everything is purely material, and that everything inexplicably came into being a really long time ago. Try as they might, they will never find the causeless cause unless they turn their attention inward. Only then do they stand a chance of discovering the timeless dimension beyond the mind. To see beyond the illusion of time and space is something anyone can easily do, and that is where the real adventure begins.

Time and space are nothing more than products of our own imagination. Although it can be argued that our ideas of time and space are rather limiting concepts, that's not to say that the world doesn't exist. It most certainly does exist, but only as an ever-changing expression and modulation of universal consciousness. The world isn't what we think it is, but we won't be able to see the reality of it as long as we continue to look at the world through the many veils created by the beliefs and conclusions we have inherited without ever questioning them. Our perception of reality is coloured not only by our beliefs and concepts, but also by the limitations of the senses and the nervous system. Consequently, neither the mind nor the senses can ever tell us what the universe really is, or even if it exists the way we think it does.

Whatever anyone says about any of this, it will only be an opinion or a piece of information, which we may choose to believe in or not, according to our conditioning. Only our own direct perception and insight can ever make any difference. Where did the world come from? When was it created? Has it always existed? Whatever anyone says about any of this may be more or less interesting or convincing, but if you are at all honest with yourself, you know very well that it's never going to be anything but mind candy. That might be okay now and again, but it is hardly sustaining in the long run.

Philosophers and thinkers have continuously entertained themselves and others down through the ages by weaving endless cobwebs of speculation around all this, but as long as the mind is looking for answers within its own limited domain of thought and memory, it is never going to understand that such questions ultimately are meaningless and have no answers, at least not on the level of mind and thought.

In the olden days, when the church was in charge of the truth, it was decided once and for all that God had created the world a really long time ago, and that was all anyone needed to know about such matters. After science had taken on the role as the messenger of truth, it was determined, after a whole lot of highfaluting discussion, that the universe started to exist by virtue of a humongous big bang, and that the dimensions of time and space were created in that very moment.

The big bang and all the explanations and complex reasoning that go with it are just more theory and speculation and can never be proven one way or the other anyway. The scientific explanation of life and the universe has actually got something in common with the religious one in the sense that it draws the conclusion that something or other for some mysterious and unfathomable reason just happened in a very remote past. Time is then usually viewed as a linear phenomenon which inexorably moves from moment to moment, all the time pushing forward into the distant future. Whether God created the universe or whether it went bump in the cosmic night is really all the same to us, isn't it? These theories are both equally limited, and they don't make the slightest bit of difference anyway.

If you really go into this and think it through properly, you will eventually realise that creation didn't happen a very long, long time ago. The universe, the world and whatever else we might think exists are continuously being created now, because there is only ever this eternal presence of now. The process of creation is life expressing itself in all its inscrutable ways and now is the timeless. There is neither beginning nor end, only a continuous and spontaneous creative unfolding. Eternity is now, this moment is forever and everything is contained within it.

The notion of time in the sense of future, present and past is continuously being created now. Everything you think that you know from the past is nothing but memories, thoughts, feelings and images spontaneously appearing now. What if you woke up one fine morning with a completely different past than the one you now think you have? In such a case you would be firmly convinced that what you were able to remember really had taken place, and this past would appear just as real as the one you now identify with. The past does not create the present, and what may seem as if it's been set in stone is constantly changing, upgrading and evolving in the eternity of now.

You might think that this seems like a rather strange kind of idea, or you might find it somewhat fascinating, but is it likely to make any kind of difference to you? It is of course up to you to accept or reject such ideas, but whether you believe this, that or the other, all beliefs, thoughts and memories exist only now. Everything you experience and ever will experience happens in this moment, and when the Grim Reaper finally arrives, he will snatch you away right now. Now is the only time there ever is, and as if that wasn't enough, this is the only place there ever is. You might have all sorts of ideas and memories about other times and places, but those ideas all exist only here and now. The scenery might appear to be constantly changing, and the clock might show all sorts of different times, but it is still always only here and now.

To some people, this might come across as bordering on mysticism, but that's fine with me. Life itself is the greatest mystery, and something that nobody will ever be able to explain or fully understand. Life is all, so I suppose you could say it is the only mystery there is, or in other words, the greatest miracle and mystery of all is existence itself.

How come life exists at all? How come anything exists? What is existence? What if nothing existed at all, not even non-existence or pure emptiness? Why is there something rather than nothing? Even trying to imagine a complete absence of the totality of life and consciousness seems impossible. How did all of this life, existence, universe, ever come into being? How can it even be possible that we are and that everything just is? Nobody truly knows what life is and the only thing anyone can ever say with certainty is, "I am," or "Consciousness is." That's all. You can't doubt that you are, or that there is indeed conscious experience, because in order to doubt or question anything, you must be here in the first place. You might not understand what you are, but your existence is a fact that can't be disputed. So while it is obviously true that I am and that consciousness is, I can't even begin to imagine how the great miracle of life is even possible, and whatever explanations I have come across, scientific, religious, spiritual or otherwise, really don't amount to much more than a rather small hill of beans once you look more closely at them.

Being is the foundation of all, and that holds true whether you seem to be in a state of deep sleep, dreaming or in the so-called waking state. What we think of as the state of deep sleep is of particular interest because in that state consciousness rests completely in itself, and there is no manifest world craving any attention. Once consciousness modulates into manifestation in the dream state, waking state and whatever other states there might be, the drama of life carries on with all its pains and pleasures. You, as the illusory separate ego-entity, are of course absent in deep sleep, but how would you even have a concept of deep dreamless sleep if there was no awareness there? You, as undifferentiated pure consciousness, are still there, otherwise you wouldn't even have a notion of the state of deep sleep. The fact that this world seems to be absent in deep sleep means nothing at all as far as your fundamental being is concerned. Awareness, consciousness, being, or whatever word you prefer to use, is always present, whether or not the world of form is on display.

But what about existence then, in the sense of the world or the universe? Do we really have any way of knowing or understanding whether it's real, what it is or what it might be for, or if it exists for any purpose at all? We might think we do, and we might have all sorts of theories to explain it all, but the stark and uncomfortable truth is that on the level of mind and thought we are all perfectly ignorant. We might talk about the big bang, or about God having created it all and come up with all sorts of fanciful ideas, but that is all just theory and speculation, stories and fairy tales. We usually take life for granted, and live our life as best we can, but that doesn't mean we understand what life is. There is a fallacy right there in how we usually think about "my" life, because that seems to imply that life is something that one has, which really is quite meaningless. We don't "have" a life; life is what we are. There is no difference between what I am, what you are and what life is. It is all one. It is all one being, one consciousness, one existence.

If the word God is to have any kind of meaning at all, it can only be as a synonym for *being*, the all-inclusive and unlimited creative conscious intelligence of life itself. God in this sense is greater, more magnificent, more omnipotent and more multidimensional than anyone could ever know or imagine. It is something that is completely and utterly beyond any kind of human understanding, and if anyone says otherwise, you can rest assured that they are seriously delusional. All the clever talk, intricate explanations and pompous pontificating in the world cannot ever get close to explaining the mystery of life, the grandeur of all existence and the glory of consciousness.

It is the only true intelligence, and it is of such magnitude that even the greatest human endeavour is utterly trivial in comparison, yet all human endeavour is obviously part of it, or an expression of it. It is just that the human mind is too small, limited and conditioned to truly grasp the totality of it. This becomes obvious just by observing nature in all its glorious splendour. Just look at what immense creativity is at play in nature. How incredibly sophisticated it all is; just thinking about the magnificent miracle of it is enough to make you feel dizzy. The human mind can't even begin to understand it and how it all works so perfectly. To me it is obvious that there is conscious, creative intelligence at work here that not only is truly miraculous but also utterly mindboggling.

Life as we know it isn't happening by chance. There is clearly intelligent design at work, but not in the sense that most people think of it; not in the sense of a God somewhere that for some inexplicable reason at some point decided to create a whole bunch of stuff. That is a very primitive and childish view of creation. Creation didn't happen in the past; creation is now. It is all now. Past, present and future are concepts created by the human mind and have no kind of objective reality. Creation is constantly unfolding, and it is synonymous with the all-inclusive conscious intelligence that is life itself.

Nature will always run its course as a perfect expression of life itself, and opposing the flow of life is pointless. You could even go so far as to say that all resistance is futile. Let life itself shape whatever is happening. Nothing can be more wasted than trying to bend life according to one's preconceived ideas and selfish desires. Just welcome life as it presents itself to you and receive all its different moods and appearances with joy and gratitude. This is the easiest thing in the world, in fact it is totally effortless, and therefore neither easy nor difficult. Just remember not to take any of it too seriously. It's just not worth it. After all, it's only a game, but a very beautiful game at that.

The beautiful gift of life is something to be cherished and welcomed with gratitude. We might not understand what life is, but that is ultimately of no great importance. Life is what we are and what everything is. It is the Great Spirit ceaselessly unfolding and manifesting in ever new ways. It is creative expression and limitless intelligence on the highest level. It is a totally spontaneous process that is always fresh, always vital, always new, always here and now.

The hard problem

In some scientific circles there is apparently a lot of debate about consciousness and its supposed origins. In these quarters the nature of consciousness and how it has come into being is sometimes referred to as the hard problem. The crux of this hard problem seems to be that it appears to be extraordinarily difficult to explain how the human brain creates consciousness. As far as I know they haven't reached any kind of meaningful or convincing conclusion to this conundrum yet, and to be honest, I don't think they ever will.

The seemingly endless discussion about the so-called hard problem is based upon a few underlying and mostly unacknowledged assumptions, and no solution to the hard problem can ever be found as long as these assumptions are not faced, examined and discarded. These assumptions are shared by virtually everyone who participates in this kind of debate, whether they are believers in religions, believers in atheism, hard-core materialists or spiritually inclined seekers. They are all fundamentally convinced that there is an objective, physical reality out there, made from something called matter, and that this reality for unknown reasons suddenly sprang into being an incredibly long time ago.

Following on from this, they also believe that this physical reality exists independently of the observer, and that we are all separate entities who somehow possess a faculty we call consciousness. The logical conclusion to this is that the human brain must somehow at some time in a distant past, for whatever reason, have developed or created consciousness, and that consciousness therefore is some kind of object that can be studied in the same way that we can study physical phenomena, emotional and mental processes and whatever else.

These assumptions are hardly ever questioned and as long as

that is the case, consciousness will continue to remain the hard problem, or whatever other fancy term the so-called experts may be able to come up with. In actual fact, this is a problem that has no true existence at all. It has come into apparent being only because of materialism's inability to explain how the brain could possibly have created consciousness. Consciousness studies are still at a very primitive level, or for the most part not really happening at all, because what is usually studied in the name of consciousness should more appropriately be referred to as studies of the mind, because that's what it actually is.

Consequently, a great deal of time, energy and passion are currently spent in the attempt to solve the hard problem and thus penetrate the enduring mystery of consciousness, and the query sometimes even takes the form of pondering whether or not consciousness might even be an illusion. Yes, believe it or not, there are highly educated people out there, sometimes with some pretty impressive credentials and mysterious looking letters after their names, who are seriously trying to convince us that consciousness is just some kind of odd misapprehension or aberration, and that it doesn't actually exist. Never mind the obvious fact that consciousness is everybody's primary and most fundamental experience, because even that can be sacrificed in the strange, convoluted process required to make the materialist worldview make sense. None of these highly educated deniers of the blatantly obvious seems to realise that their outlandish ideas must necessarily appear within consciousness in the first place, otherwise how would there even be any awareness of them?

Consciousness is quite clearly the big fat festering carbuncle on the end of the long nose of materialism. It is the one thing that none of the long-nosed materialists can ever explain away, that they cannot get rid of, no matter how hard they are trying. Claiming that consciousness doesn't actually exist at all, that it's all an illusion, is of course so totally irrational that it's impossible for anyone reasonably intelligent and open-minded to take it seriously. Not only is materialism the most absurd and far-fetched philosophy the human mind has ever conceived, but the attempts by some of materialism's most hard-core fundamentalist fanatics to deny the very existence and reality of consciousness is downright bizarre. It is in fact a denial of their own reality, existence and first-hand experience, and that plainly doesn't make any sense at all. It can even be argued that the kind of reasoning presented by the high priests of contemporary materialist philosophy is a kind of intellectual insanity, or at the very least that it is a desperate, futile and laughable attempt at denying what's plainly obvious just because it won't fit into their cherished faith of materialist philosophy. It's all totally illogical and ridiculous of course, but if nothing else, all this hullaballoo about the hard problem and the supposed non-existence of consciousness proves that there is a mighty fine collection of highly distinguished idiots out there, people who are educated way beyond and far above their rather modest level of intelligence.

Then there are also those who are seriously considering if consciousness might be present in the universe as a fundamental kind of property or element. This point of view may seem reasonable enough, but the argument is framed incorrectly because consciousness isn't just an aspect of life, like gravity, electricity, magnetism, matter and so on. Consciousness is the infinite, eternal totality in which gravity, matter and everything else appear, seem to exist and disappear. Thinking about consciousness along these lines, as if it is some kind of part or property of all material things and beings, indicates that consciousness is seen as just another facet of reality, a feature of the universe so to speak.

This kind of belief is sometimes referred to as panpsychism, but it is essentially just a cleverly designed version of materialism. Although it acknowledges consciousness, at least in a fashion, it is still firmly anchored in the fundamental misunderstanding caused by assuming that what is thought of as the material universe has objective reality independent of consciousness, and that all forms of life somehow have something called consciousness. It would actually be more correct to say that nothing or nobody has consciousness, and that all forms and living beings are unique modulations, manifestations and expressions of consciousness.

Consciousness is not only absolutely fundamental, but it is also the indivisible and basic reality in which all aspects of the universe and all possible universes appear and disappear. The idea that consciousness somehow resides within the various forms of matter is a major misapprehension, which leads to nothing but confusion and increasing levels of ignorance, because it starts with matter as the ultimate reality and then adds consciousness to it. No evidence exists for matter or any other forms of life being fundamental or ultimately real, so the entire materialist worldview is based solely on belief and speculation and has little or nothing to do with reality. Materialism is like a dying duck desperately trying to quack; in other words not very convincing at all. It just doesn't stand up to serious scrutiny and is long overdue for being thrown on to the ever increasing scrapheap of utterly useless intellectual claptrap.

The fact is that science in spite of its best efforts has not come anywhere near explaining how the brain generates awareness and conscious experience, and as long as all those bright and clever scientific minds are trying to solve this hard problem within a purely materialistic framework they won't ever be able to find any kind of solution to it. The reason for that is of course that the brain doesn't generate consciousness at all, and as long as scientists or other experts start from the assumption that consciousness is a by-product of some kind of brain activity, they will never understand what consciousness is. It will forever remain the hard problem because consciousness cannot be understood or explained on the purely conceptual or intellectual level.

The human brain and nervous system can more realistically be seen as necessary tools for universal consciousness to experience itself and life in human form. To believe that the brain creates consciousness is equivalent to believing that a cinema screen is creating the images in a movie, or that whatever nonsense that you watch on your television is somehow created by the television set itself. The TV and the cinema screen are both just tools for allowing us to have the kind of experiences that we have as spectators, and do not themselves create anything at all.

The current materialistic paradigm states that the physical brain creates or generates consciousness from physical matter and chemical processes, and thus it logically follows that our entire existence is confined to the period of time between birth and death. Within the paradigm of materialism there is no other possibility of explaining the emergence of consciousness than to say that some sort of material stuff somehow created conscious experience. This is of course totally absurd and proves that science is pretty much completely in the dark when it comes to understanding or explaining the mystery and nature of consciousness. For all of science's vast knowledge about the brain's physiology and how it functions, not even the top scientific minds of neuroscience can offer any kind of reasonable or valid explanation of what consciousness is, where it came from or how it emerged.

The idea of the brain as the creator of consciousness is clearly absurd. It might be closer to the truth to define or describe the brain as a kind of filtering mechanism. It can be viewed as a mechanism that somehow steps down the unimaginable totality of universal consciousness to something that can be handled by the human nervous system and organism, reducing it to what we normally consider our day-to-day normal experience, or normal human awareness in the here and now. When seen from this point of view, so-called anomalous experiences like out-of-body experiences, near-death experiences, remote viewing, telepathy, precognition, past life recall, clairvoyance and so on can be explained as a kind of partial access to a much wider and more thorough view of reality.

It is important to understand that consciousness isn't an object that can be measured, quantified, defined or described because that would necessarily impose limitations on it. Consciousness cannot be categorised or pigeonholed in any way whatsoever. It is the eternal, infinite, all-encompassing, inscrutable reality in which all manner of manifestation is played out, and therefore without definition or attributes that can be attached to it. All phenomena are made from consciousness alone, they are all expressions of consciousness, whether it's on the material, mental, emotional, psychic, astral, or any other level. All phenomena thus depend totally on consciousness for without consciousness nothing whatsoever could ever exist. Yet consciousness doesn't depend on anything. It is what it is, irrespective of manifestation or not.

There is an infinite variety of states of mind, but there are no states of consciousness. Consciousness is beyond all states, beyond all experience, beyond all manifestation. It was never born and will never die. It is the causeless cause, the true source of all that is. It is the ultimate reality beyond the mental constructs of time and space. It is what you truly are, and peace on Earth will effortlessly spring forth from that realisation.

Once you realise that your true identity is pure, limitless, universal, unchanging, ordinary consciousness – that which is aware of these words and their meaning – then everything else becomes clear, and the hard problem and similar highfaluting mumbo-jumbo are seen for what they are: "Much ado about nothing". The hard problem was thought up by the human mind, and all the talk, debate, discussion, arguing and pontificating in the world won't solve it, for the simple reason that it doesn't actually exist. It is just a mind construct. Consciousness alone forever remains. Everything else comes and goes, and is ultimately of no more importance or significance than little soft ripples on the surface of infinite oceans of possibility and potentiality.

The unity of science and spirituality

Some clever dude once said that the difference between religion and spirituality is that religion provides answers that may never be questioned whereas spirituality asks questions that may never be answered. There is a great deal of truth in that, even though many people may never even have reflected upon the difference between the two. It is very important to realise though that there really is a difference, especially so in light of the ongoing dispute between religion and science as to who has the right answers to the most fundamental questions of life.

In this debate, it would appear that the scientific view has pretty much demolished the religious one. Science seems to have won this discussion, and although the scientific argument has effectively exposed the religious point of view as a fanciful fairy tale, it hasn't managed to come up with any sensible and convincing answers to the deepest and most enduring questions of life. In terms of presenting a meaningful and satisfying worldview, science has come up short, and never given us any real answers to life's most fundamental questions.

Science has in a sense taken over religion's role as the keeper of truth, but as far as I can tell, science and religion have more in common than most people think. It can't be disputed that science in the course of the last few centuries has taken over much of the role that religions used to play, and in some ways developed into what appears to be contemporary society's most cherished belief system. It could even be argued that science is a new kind of religion or at the very least provides a kind of belief system and worldview that many people seem to be comfortable with.

Scientists have taken on the role as the high priests of our age. When the Church was in charge of everything, it must have been very difficult or even dangerous to question the

Christian worldview. Those few courageous individuals who first did that had to fight a laborious and risky battle to make the new scientific worldview heard. At that time, science was young, new, creative and innovative, and at its best it is of course still creative and innovative, but it's an undeniable fact that dogmatic and rigid thinking has become part of the picture as well. It is unfortunately not exactly uncommon for many scientists to display much the same dogmatism and arrogance that organised religion all too often has been so full of.

Science claims to be exploring reality in an objective manner, but its spokespersons are often as prejudiced as anyone else. This is illustrated brilliantly every time the accepted scientific worldview is challenged by people who dare to think along new and creative lines. That is of course no fault of science itself, but just a predictable result of the current ego-based way in which the human mind often tends to operate.

It is obvious that most of us suffer from an unnecessary fear of anything that goes against our pet cherished beliefs, and there is no reason to think that scientists and other highly educated people would be an exception to this. After all, it's often the case that anything that's not considered to be in line with the basic doctrines of science is often ridiculed and debunked as superstition, imagination or escapism. If something can't be measured, quantified and rationally explained, it often seems unacceptable to mainstream science, and while there is no reason to accept anything uncritically, putting on scientific blinkers doesn't do much good either.

The methodology of science has added something very valuable to human consciousness by encouraging logic and critical examination instead of religious belief and superstitious dogma. This has to some extent freed us from the tyranny of religion, but in spite of this, it seems to me that the scientifically founded model of life is no more satisfying than religion and theology in terms of providing convincing answers to the most fundamental questions of life.

I am not suggesting that science can be reduced to the same level as religion when it comes to understanding life. At least in terms of methodology it may well be a lot more sophisticated and advanced than any of the religions, but on the other hand, think about the underlying worldview of mainstream science, the paradigm that science presently seems to be operating within. It is not that much more advanced than that of any bog standard religion.

The predominantly materialistic worldview of science has given us the utterly absurd idea of a soulless and mechanistic universe that is totally devoid of meaning, and completely governed by blind, automatic, mechanical forces. In this universe nothing but what can be measured and quantified exists. Everything is explained as being a result of physical and chemical processes, and nature has been reduced to an advanced machine. As if the boundless creativity, order and intelligence of life could be some kind of unconscious and ultra-sophisticated clockwork that accidentally just happens to work absolutely perfectly. And as if that wasn't enough, materialism disguised as science maintains that the wondrous, mysterious and inexplicable life that we are all expressions of has arisen as a result of sheer luck and the unconscious play of coincidental blind forces over billions of years of evolution towards ever higher forms of life. This curious idea is one of reductionist science's most cherished myths, but that doesn't prevent it from being as far out on the wrong limb as the Christian thesis that God created the world in six days and rested on the seventh.

All such explanations are of course totally meaningless, because they are based on nothing but unchallenged suppositions and ready-made conclusions. Atheism and hard-core materialism have to a large extent taken over the position of the religious beliefs of bygone times, but it is a worldview that represents a stubborn, prejudiced and extremely limited way of relating to the mystery of life and existence. I would go so far as to say that a belief in atheism is even more primitive and ridiculous than a belief in God, because the idea of God at the very least is a pale reflection of truth, whereas atheism amounts to nothing more than a pathetic declaration of spiritual bankruptcy.

By the way, I have nothing against atheism, or any other kind of belief for that matter, and to me it doesn't matter whether people think of themselves as atheists or not. What's important are your personal qualities, and to what extent you manifest kindness, generosity and compassion in your life. We are hopefully all doing that to some extent, but it doesn't depend on whether we are religious, atheists or subscribe to any other kind of belief system. The love you express and manifest on a daily basis is the only thing that is of any consequence, because only love can change the world for the better and truly make a difference.

What we consciously or unconsciously are looking for or expect to find is often exactly what reveals itself to us. Everybody who believes in something will always maintain that they know and will often find what appears to be indisputable proof of what they are already convinced of. No matter what we choose to believe in, we will often search for anything that can confirm our beliefs and overlook whatever doesn't fit.

Many scientists and researchers deliberately or otherwise focus on what supports their own theories and overlook whatever doesn't fit their worldview. This has been demonstrated time and time again, and what I'm saying about belief, projection and expectation also holds true for scientists. Most people's worldview is to a great extent based on subjective notions, prejudiced opinions and whatever conclusions might be in fashion, and people within the field of science aren't any different in that respect. It is not that uncommon for scientists not only to overlook anything that goes against their beliefs, but also to try and suppress and counteract anything that constitutes a threat to their own version of reality. The definition of reality adopted by science is in a way very narrow-minded, precisely because it is usually limited to what can be quantified, measured, classified and verbally explained.

This attitude is so universally dominant that man's intellect and rationality now govern the world almost completely. Our intellectual abilities are of course very useful, but there is no reason to take what is nothing more than a valuable tool and turn it into something akin to a deity. In our modern materialistic culture our intuitive, psychic, spiritual and creative faculties have to a great extent been pushed aside. Intellectual capacity has become synonymous with intelligence, even though the intellect is only a small part of a much bigger reality.

It is fairly common to think that a university degree and a sharp, analytical intellect are proof of intelligence, but this is sheer nonsense. After all, scientists who use their resources, skills and knowledge to develop ever more deadly and monstrous weapons can hardly be called intelligent. The same goes for those who torture and kill defenceless animals in laboratories, all in the name of science and progress. Those who engage in such utterly cruel acts only prove that they are lacking in empathy and compassion, and are willing slaves of the establishment and its demands. They may be dutiful and obedient, but also more or less completely brainwashed by a system that is built from sheer self-centredness, greed and fear By uncritically accepting the blatant lies and phoney ideals we have all been spoon-fed for so long, they have also betrayed whatever intelligence they may still have.

Being intelligent has very little to do with intellectual cleverness and cramming as much information as possible into your head. Intelligence means that you have an intuitive ability to see the entirety of an issue instead of focusing on just one particular aspect or even cutting it all into little pieces.

Intelligence connects the dots so that you can see the bigger picture so to speak. Therefore you also have a much greater capacity to respond from a state of wholeness instead of just relying on a belief system or a limited and often prejudiced point of view. Even more importantly, intelligence is distinguished by compassion for all life and a capacity for unconditional love. And if there is one thing that the world is lacking today it must certainly be love.

Technological progress can undeniably be a source of great blessings, and in many ways that has been the case over the last few centuries. However, as long as we are not sufficiently intelligent to utilise technology in a sensible and sensitive manner, it will more often than not turn into a curse. The bottom line is that no matter what advanced technology science develops, by its very nature it doesn't bring more love, harmony and intelligence into the world. It can't, because it's really nothing more than a tool. Without intelligence and compassion, we are destined for conflict and degradation, eventually leading to a painful and pitiful demise of our civilisation.

Advanced technology is not an end in itself, and if it is turned into a goal for its own sake, it will ultimately prove to be a dead end. Our love affair with technology has blinded us and seems to be making us more stupid day by day. Technology has become so important to the vast majority of us that it has turned into a cultural obsession. It's something that seems so absolutely essential to virtually every single aspect of our lives that most of us couldn't even imagine life without it.

We have made ourselves incredibly dependent on fancy gadgets and high-tech wizardry, but the more we are doing that, the more we are also losing touch with the natural world and the blessed Earth. This has exposed our entire civilisation to great danger, and made us extremely vulnerable, both as individuals and as a species, because even if technology can bring us great benefits if it is used wisely, it is also very fragile and prone to malfunctioning. For example, it wouldn't take more than a big enough solar flare to bring down the entire world wide web of electronic connections, which of course would have catastrophic consequences for virtually everybody. The only people whose lives wouldn't necessarily be affected by such a scenario are the relatively few humans who still haven't entered the electronic and digital age. They are the very small minority still living in close communion with nature without access to any kind of electronics or wireless technology, such as indigenous and tribal people in some isolated parts of the world. And after all is said and done, it may well be these so-called primitive people who will inherit the new Earth.

The disadvantage of our civilisation's modern version of the dance around the golden calf is that it can never lead to any real fulfilment, and that it pulls us ever further away from the natural world and the sanctity of life. It increasingly makes us live in a kind of virtual reality, which makes true and honest communication more and more difficult. Human beings can in the long run never be at ease with life in a totally secularised, materialistic and atheistic world where everything is based on technology, material values and flimsy pleasures. The need to penetrate deeper into the mysteries of life and find true fulfilment can never be totally suppressed, because everybody has an inclination towards living life in unity with the consciousness that is the source and essence of all of life.

Everybody will sooner or later discover that there are no solutions or answers outside themselves, and that all explanations are ultimately worthless. The traditional religions are for all practical purposes nothing more than living corpses, all the political ideologies in the world are only meaningless waffle and the intellectual materialism of science hasn't got much more to offer than a universe bereft of consciousness, intelligence, purpose and meaning. Neither politics, religion nor science has managed to come up with solutions to the many problems we are facing today or answers to the fundamental questions human beings everywhere have always asked themselves.

A good example of this is the question of the original causeless cause of life and existence. What could possibly have set it all into motion? Materialist philosophy claims that the so-called big bang was the origin, but if everything was created or set into motion by the big bang, what was the cause of that in the first place? On the other hand, Christian theology tells us that God created the world and everything in it a good long while ago, but what could possibly have made God do such a thing? And why would he do it at the particular time that it's supposed to have happened? Irrespective of what kind of worldview, belief or cosmology one subscribes to, one always comes up against this kind of question, and it's a question that appears to have no satisfying or convincing answer within the existing paradigm of science, religion or philosophy.

We can ponder and discuss such questions until the cowgirls come home, but the reality that we are confronted with on a daily basis is that the world is stark raving mad. This madness has its root in man's psyche, centred in our monumental lack of self-knowledge. The activities we are involved in, whether they are concerned with politics, science, religion or whatever else, are to a great extent expressions of the neuroses the vast majority of us are all overflowing with.

The only thing that can ever make a difference to the runaway insanity presently on display in the world is a radical transformation of human consciousness, which can only happen through the individual. Such a transformation is now an urgent necessity, but it cannot be imposed collectively from somewhere else or from some imaginary God. It can only become a reality when spontaneously emerging from deep within consciousness, as expressed through each and every one of us. Unless this happens, all attempts at finding fulfilment or improving the world are ultimately doomed to fail. A revolution in the deepest part of our psyche is necessary if anything is to change at all, other than on very superficial levels. Anything else amounts to nothing more than chasing after the wind.

It's easy enough to see that this is the case, but what difference can it ever make what anyone thinks, writes or says about any of it? No matter how much we argue, discuss, debate, analyse, pontificate, think and believe, whatever we are able to come up with more often than not remains nothing more than empty bubble-talk that's not capable of changing anything. It is of course standard procedure for many of us to try and convince others of our knowledge and intellectual excellence, but how many of us are aware of how wasted all our intellectual claptrap really is? Not a single ounce of what is continuously running out of our mouths has the power to trigger the spiritual transformation that has now become an absolutely crucial necessity for humanity and life on Earth to survive. The only thing that can ever make a real difference is the quality of consciousness expressed through each individual human being. In other words, if you are free from violence, fear and greed, and live in harmony, peace and love, you are already changing the world for the better. No further action is required, although action may very well be taken if you feel moved to do so. Yes, it really is as simple as that.

In spite of the enormous contribution of science to human development and welfare, it is obvious that it has come to an impasse in terms of providing realistic and convincing answers to the most fundamental questions of life. Science has unfortunately become stuck in a materialistic paradigm that is preventing it from moving ahead and penetrating deeper in its quest for understanding life and the universe. It is now imperative that science discards its irrational belief in materialism and takes on board a spiritual view of life. Spirituality is not opposed to science in the way that religion seems to be. It is completely compatible with the ethos of science and the scientific method, and the inevitable merging of science and spirituality will be a blessing for all of us, and also an essential ingredient in humanity's further development and full flowering as a species.

If we try to define a spiritual way of life, we will realise that it is not that different from the scientific approach. After all, true spirituality aims for ever deeper insight, increased knowledge and is also based entirely on direct experience, not on the blind belief of religion. It is intellectually honest, open to the possibility of being mistaken, and ideally also completely free from any kind of evangelism and superstition. The spiritual quest and way of life accepts and relishes a state of not knowing, of being open to whatever truth may eventually emerge. This is all not only compatible with science, but could even be seen as a good definition of science itself, yet most materialistically-minded scientists would probably find it next to impossible to see any connection between what they are doing and a spiritual way of life.

The problem is that most scientists have automatically accepted a materialistic worldview which is based purely on speculation and theory. Many of the most cherished assumptions on which the underlying scientific worldview is based are hardly ever questioned. The materialistic dogma of something called physical matter being the fundamental reality of life has been accepted blindly not only by most scientists, but also by most people, regardless of what they might otherwise believe in. A belief in atheism is so prevalent that at least in some parts of the world it is now the most common form of philosophy. The belief that life is built from matter only, and that everything else has evolved from that, is taken as proven fact, even though there is absolutely no evidence for it whatsoever. It logically follows from this belief system that consciousness, mind and all human experience are somehow all extensions to or have been created from physical matter, which clearly is impossible, because how can the various bits and pieces of matter ever give rise to conscious experience? What would be the impetus for such a development in the first place? How could there ever be any kind of development or evolution at all if inert matter is all there ever is, was and will be?

The scientific method is of course tremendously valuable, and must necessarily involve questioning everything, including even the most cherished and basic assumptions on which science itself seems to rest. This is presently for the most part not the case. The basic philosophical foundation of materialism, from which most scientists operate, is not questioned. Instead it is taken for granted, accepted on faith, that matter is all that exists, all that is real, and that everything else arises from that. According to materialist philosophy, all conscious experience, all thought, all feeling and emotion, all awareness and sense of being are somehow, through some mysterious unknown process, created by the brain. In other words, it's all a derivative of matter. A much more realistic way of looking at the mystery of life is to acknowledge that all perceptions, thoughts, experiences, sensations, feelings and so on are all unfolding within the supreme intelligence of universal consciousness. Everything is a modulation or expression of the Great Spirit of Life itself. There is no other reality, nothing separate, or outside of this oneness that is all, and it could even be described as consciousness being conscious of itself.

It is now imperative that science and scientists gather the courage, wisdom and intelligence to leave the materialistic worldview behind. What is necessary is to take the quantum leap into a new dimension, in which consciousness is acknowledged as the source of all life, and in which everything that exists on the level of form is seen as a manifestation of universal consciousness. This more spiritual view and way of life must become its new mode, and science must unreservedly embrace spirituality as the vital missing link in the scientific method and understanding of life. Until that happens further developments in science can only be towards splitting life into smaller and smaller units, gaining more and more relative understanding of how the various parts of life seem to relate to one another, and thus finding ever more clever ways of expanding technology and eventually making us all redundant.

This kind of ongoing reductionist process may seem like a very exciting and promising development for many of us, but none of it can ever break the spells of materialistic dogmatism and atheism that are keeping science and humanity from evolving towards a true understanding of what life is and why we are here in the first place. A materialistic worldview and way of life will never be able to create a world free from conflict, environmental devastation and ever more superficial ways of living. The absurd and ridiculous belief in materialism must be discarded in favour of authentic spiritual understanding and a spiritual way of life, which means a way of life and a way of conducting science that are based on generosity, harmony, and cooperation.

Science has the potential to evolve into a true guiding light for humanity, but only after fully and wholeheartedly merging with spirituality and taking to heart a genuinely spiritual view of life. Only then will we be able to move towards a way of life and a reality which may prove to be more creative, glorious and fulfilling than any of us could ever have imagined. That means that we have the potential to create and embody a way of life and reality in which God is no longer a blind and superstitious belief, but an obvious and living reality for every one of us. And if that ever happens, the word God will have served its purpose, and may thus be discarded for good.

A new Earth

Humanity seems currently to be on a course to making itself redundant, while destroying nature and the beautiful Earth in the process. This process is of course entirely unnecessary and absolutely reversible, but can only be turned around by a revolution at the very core of the human psyche, which would in effect be nothing short of a spiritual awakening of global proportions. The rebirth of humanity and the dawn of a new Earth can be a reality only if each and every one of us goes through a fundamental inner change, and it is a change that will take us from fear to love, conflict to harmony and separation to unity. Until that happens we are destined to repeat the same old mistakes, and basically just find ever new ways of exploiting and hurting ourselves and each other, nature and the world.

We all have an intuitive feeling that the world could be a lot better, more harmonious and peaceful than it presently is, but hardly anybody seems to have much of an inkling as to how that could come about. The first thing we need to realise in this context is that the world isn't something that exists independently of us. For better or worse, it is our own creation and our own joint responsibility. The world is essentially the people inhabiting it and their relationships with each other, because that's what makes the world into whatever it is. It is all too easy to become depressed about the state of the world, and the horror and insanity of it all, but what is that insanity and horror other than a reflection of the current state of the human psyche?

It is no exaggeration to say that we live in a world that is predominantly run by fear and greed, which means that it is run by selfishness. All too many of us expect politicians or other people in power to solve the world's problems, but that's doing nothing more than disclaiming responsibility for our own lives.

This is tantamount to turning our backs on the madness we are all responsible for, but this attitude is typical of the mentality most of us seem to have adopted. It is always somebody else who has brought about the world's misfortunes, and it is always somebody else's responsibility to do something about them. It is easy enough to point one's finger at politicians and people in power, and designate them as the main culprits of the many miseries of the world. While many of them are obviously guilty of serious crimes against the people they are supposed to be serving, blaming them doesn't solve any problems.

It has been said that we get the political leaders we deserve and there is some truth in that. The presidents, prime ministers and whoever else we think are in power aren't that much different from the rest of us. They might have a position in society that is very different from anything most of us will ever experience, but their quality of mind and heart is more or less the same as that of most everybody else. In fact, people in high places of power will often have been corrupted to such a degree that they are significantly more destructive and selfish than the average person. After all, power corrupts, and absolute power corrupts absolutely.

The vast majority of people still live in the grip of ego, seeing themselves as separate entities engaged in a seemingly ceaseless struggle for survival. Living in this way, we all want to grab as much as we can for ourselves, without much consideration for the common good of all. Why would political leaders and other influential people be any different? They're not of course, and in many ways may even be more greedy and cunning than the rest of us. You'd be hard pressed to find a single person moving in the top circles of politics, business, finance, media or the corporate world who is speaking and acting from a place of true compassion, understanding, harmony and love. It would be naïve to expect to find any sane person in a position of real power and influence. More often than not, it is of course nothing but ruthless ambition and pure selfishness that has enabled people in power to ascend to the most elevated positions of society in the first place.

For some inexplicable reason a lot of people are still buying into the idea that new political leadership will bring about change, that we should be strong in our belief in a better world, and fervently hope that somehow it's magically going to come about. This is just an illusion, and history has shown us time and again that it hardly ever happens. All politicians the world over have always promised that everything will change for the better as soon as they get into power, but the fact is that nothing much ever changes in this way. If we want more enlightened and compassionate politicians and leaders we ourselves are going to have to be more enlightened and compassionate. I think it was Gandhi who once said that we have to be the change that we want to see in the world and this is absolutely true. A world without fear, greed, poverty, exploitation, conflict and war is certainly possible, but can only come about through each individual manifesting the qualities of love, harmony, freedom and peace in his or her own life.

It goes without saying that an inner revolution of immense proportions will have to occur for the world out there to change to one of peace and harmony. At the present time it is obvious that people living a life free from fear and greed are in a very small minority, and the world reflects this perfectly. However, if and when a radical revolution in human consciousness does take place on a grand scale, the world will be transformed accordingly. That's what it's going to take.

This is not to say that we might as well not bother trying to correct what is wrong in the world, and I'm most certainly not suggesting that all social and political activism is pointless. The crucial factor in this respect is where that activism is coming from and what quality is at its centre. An individual who has reached spiritual maturity may well be moved to instigate and carry out social and political action, but without an inner foundation of peace and harmony any such action will only perpetuate the current state of affairs and bring about even more misery. Whenever we feel moved to help others in need, disseminate information or campaign for causes we feel strongly about, we can honour that impulse and still do a lot of good in the world as long as the motivation arises from a state of compassion and wisdom, and not from one of vanity and selfishness.

What is more important than anything else is to realise the urgent need for a fundamental transformation of human consciousness. In the long run, this is the only solution to humanity's problems, and the only thing that can bring about real change in the world. Spiritual transformation is not an abstract idea or a fancy notion dreamt up by some philosopher or guru somewhere. It is quite simply the transmutation of fear into love, greed into generosity, competition into cooperation, conflict into harmony, war into peace and separation into oneness. This needs to happen on the level of the individual, and therefore we are all directly and personally responsible for the creation of a new Earth built on a creative foundation of peace, love, harmony and freedom. The essential ingredient necessary for this to happen is the full realisation of oneself as universal consciousness and the oneness of all life. Unless this realisation is a living reality for us, any talk about change and reform will remain nothing but fancy words that mean next to nothing.

We already know very well what we are doing as a species and where it is all heading, and we could easily change our irrational and destructive ways if we really wanted to. However, it is not so much a question of which precautions we ought to take to prevent a sweeping, full-scale destruction of nature and the end of civilisation as we know it. The only thing that can put a definite end to our relentless exploitation of nature and each other is a fundamental change within each and every one of us. Many people might think that a statement like that is just too naïve and simplistic, but such a change would automatically create the necessary foundation to solve whatever social, political and environmental problems we are facing now. The source of the challenges facing humanity lies hidden within the human psyche, but only a few people, relatively speaking, have come to realise that a deep-rooted spiritual revolution is the only thing that can ever change anything at all.

During the last couple of centuries we have brought about an impressive technological revolution, but we have as yet not gone through the psychological and spiritual change that is necessary to be able to utilise this technology in a sensitive and sensible way. To exaggerate just a teeny little bit for once, I would say that when it comes to spiritual maturity, most of us appear to be still living in the Stone Age. In all our modernism, affluence and success we are still fundamentally as greedy, selfish and violent as we have always been. As long as this is the case, we will also necessarily continue the destruction of ourselves, each other and this beautiful Earth.

It doesn't seem at all likely that an inner transformation of the magnitude I'm talking about is going to happen anytime soon. An overwhelming majority of humanity is quite simply neither interested in discovering the truth about themselves nor in changing how they relate to others and the world. Quite the contrary, as a species we seem adamant in our efforts to trigger a full-blown global catastrophe, and for all I know, such shock treatment may soon be the only possible course of action left for humanity. There is even a possibility that we might already have gone too far to prevent such an unpleasant scenario from manifesting itself. Still, there is no reason to despair, because our brutality, cruelty, ignorance and stupidity will never go so far as to completely wipe out life on Earth. The essence of life is creativity, intelligence, beauty and love, and these qualities will always be much more powerful than whatever insanity and folly we are able to come up with.

Humankind's most fundamental challenges are of a psychological and spiritual nature. It is naïve to believe that the problems confronting us can be solved without a drastic inner revolution taking place. We all contribute to the madness that has descended upon the world, and it goes without saying that as long as most of us live a life based on conflict, selfishness, fear and greed, the world is bound to reflect that perfectly, which is exactly what it does.

The origin of all social and political turmoil, of all environmental problems and of all wars can be found in the individual's own inner conflicts, which is a direct result of living one's life through a false ego-based identity. Virtually everyone is caught up in some kind of conflict within him- or herself, and whoever is in a state of inner conflict is also going to be at odds with their surroundings. This spreads throughout the world faster than bad news, and the result is a world that has become an inferno of madness and suffering.

Most people seem to be unaware of the fact that they are responsible for what the world is, and even if you tell them, they are unlikely to see and accept this simple fact. For the most part, we take for granted that the world is separate from what we are, but the fact is that each and every one of us *is* the world. The misery we have created in the world has its roots within us. Whether we live in love and harmony or conflict and fear, we can't avoid giving our contribution to society and the world as a whole through our quality of heart and mind. Whoever wants to change the world for the better will have to live in peace with themselves and their surroundings. There are no two ways about it.

The way the world is now, we are witnessing conflict and discord pretty much in all areas, and it is all a result of our lack of self-knowledge, inner disharmony and sheer insanity. The structure of society and the general conditions of the world are the direct results of the conflicts most of us are constantly creating within ourselves and with others. Our selfishness and greed cannot fail to make the world into a hotbed for war, conflicts, corruption and abuse of power, whereas harmonious, peaceful and loving people would naturally and quite effortlessly create a world overflowing with love, peace and harmony.

If you doubt that this is the case and find it hard to accept, it just means that you haven't thought it through properly. I don't know if it might help you to grasp this, but as a little experiment, just try to imagine that everybody all over the world suddenly stopped killing and stealing. Don't you think that this would make a colossal difference? Wouldn't the world be transformed as if by magic? The effect would be enormous, but still, these are just minor matters. It is not really such a big deal to avoid taking other people's lives or possessions, although for some people it may seem close to impossible. The only real obstacle is that we don't want to let go of our self-centred and destructive ways of life, hence the world is the way it is.

Whether one lives in a quagmire of ignorance and spiritual poverty or manifests a harmonious life based on wisdom and love is ultimately each person's own choice and responsibility. In terms of solving the world's problems, politics and ideologies are nothing more than the pitiful results of our endless confusion and self-centredness. Contrary to what many people may think, the solution to mankind's problems does not lie in some ideology or political system, but within each and every one of us. Within us all there is an inexhaustible fountain of love and creativity, and once we allow this divine fountain to nourish and feed our lives, the world will be transformed accordingly.

As this is being written, during the second decade of the 21st century, we are witnessing an increasing trend towards globalisation, centralisation of power in all areas, massively increased surveillance, a shocking loss of civil liberties and a seemingly endless number of new laws, rules and regulations being imposed on people all over the world. This trend has as its logical end result a world in which all power is concentrated in the hands of a tiny elite of megalomaniac globalists, with the means to total surveillance and complete control over everybody.

This would essentially be an undiluted expression of fascism on a global scale, and it would of course all be justified as being implemented for the common good of all. In reality though, this kind of scenario is nothing more than the ego's ultimate power trip fantasy and the pitiful and tragic final goal of a mind-set that is operating exclusively through selfishness and greed. To most of us such a world doesn't seem very attractive at all, but how many of us are willing to take a stand for freedom and human dignity? How many of us will refuse to comply with all the harassment and nonsense we are asked to accept in the name of health, safety and security?

We may think that we have no desire for power, but once we start to observe ourselves carefully during daily life and become aware of how we interact with others, we will, if we are honest with ourselves, be able to see the fight for power and control being played out in our own lives. The human mind is full of desire to have everything its own way. We all know this from our own experience, and it shouldn't be too difficult to realise that this inevitably leads to conflict with other people whose desires tend to be at odds with our own. You can easily see this for yourself in little things like wanting to be right, insisting on deciding how to do things when dealing with others and defending our right to have it our way, regardless of how it affects other people.

These are all very small things of course, seemingly all quite innocent, but it is on this very personal level that conflict starts, before it impacts the environment and the society we happen to be part of and eventually joins all the other little conflicts constantly being created by virtually everybody. And thus our petty little conflicts and disharmonies will all sooner or later help to contribute to whatever global problems we're facing, just like many small brooks, streams and tributaries all contribute to the majestic flow of a mighty river.

The simple fact is that the world is never going to change for the better unless the individual changes, and if each of us goes through an inner transformation, the world will necessarily change of its own accord. Consequently, all discussion about what an ideal world ought to look like or how it should be organised or structured is ultimately pointless. This much I know though: In a sane world, there are no such things as politics and politicians, armies, police, prisons, mega-corporations, banking cartels and stock markets. I could of course have added many other things to this list, but I think you get the gist of what I mean by this. The point is that all of this stuff can survive only in a world run by fear, greed and selfishness, because that is the necessary fuel for all of it.

Isn't it obvious that a sane world necessarily would have to be inhabited by people who live in peace, freedom, love and harmony? In other words, people who are actually sane. Why would they ever need any of the things I just mentioned? All of these things would seem utterly pointless to people living in a sane world, and none of it would even be seriously considered by anyone. Consequently, it would all be considered redundant and eventually forgotten, because a spiritually mature humanity would have no desire or need for dwelling on humanity's past errors, misdeeds and tragedies.

This might seem a tad far-fetched to some people, maybe even completely surreal, but that's only because we are so used to all of those things, and a lot more nonsense besides, and most of us would probably find it almost impossible even to visualise a world where peace reigns supreme. Moreover, isn't it obvious that a world created and controlled by selfishness and rampant insanity completely depends on politicians, police, armies, corporations, blatant systemic financial exploitation, and all the rest of it to function at all?

Insanity is so pervasive these days that it has in fact become quite normal, and whatever is normal is almost automatically considered sane. But if you stop and think about it for a minute, or however much time you may need, you will realise that what is normal is not necessarily sane. Just to take one example, let's consider armies and the whole idea of armed forces and defence. At the present time, there are soldiers and armies in virtually every country on Earth, and this has been the state of affairs for millennia, so it is all quite normal. However, their business is obviously that of war, isn't it? Now, can you honestly think of anything more totally and utterly insane than war?

I know that many people would say that we have armed forces to protect ourselves and to create peace, and I know there are so-called peacekeeping forces and whatever other euphemistic terms they may come up with, but none of it has anything to do with peace. Thinking that you can create or secure peace by making yourself ready for war or engaging in acts of war makes just about as much sense as fornicating for virginity. It just doesn't work.

The issue at hand is that armies either fight wars or prepare themselves for wars. What could possibly be more totally bonkers than war? Not much as far as I can see. Wars have been fought all over the world and for all sorts of reasons for thousands of years, but have armies and wars ever brought peace? Maybe in the sense that when a war ends, there is a temporary absence of hostilities, but other than that, war brings only misery, death and destruction, and never peace. Armies fight battles and engage in wars, or make sure that they're ready for them, which is most certainly not conducive to peace at all.

Armed conflict is such a common occurrence that it could be considered perfectly normal, but that doesn't change the fact that war is in reality a state sponsored act of murder and a kind of organised insanity. It is also quite normal to think that there is an enemy out there somewhere that we need to defend ourselves against. We are constantly being brainwashed into believing such nonsense, but if there is any kind of enemy at all, it is within. Humanity is one, we are all in the same boat, and we have no other enemies than our own fear, greed, ignorance and stupidity.

The idea that there is a group of people or nations that are potential or real enemies is a most unfortunate misunderstanding. It is universally accepted that this is how it is, but that doesn't make it true or any more meaningful. And what about the so-called war on terror? It's all a ruse to keep the majority of the population controlled through fear of a projected external enemy. At the moment this seems to be quite successful, but once you declare war on anything, you have already admitted defeat. The so-called war on terror is in reality based on a rapacious lust for power and control, which of course is a very effective barrier to peace, and as long as the world is run primarily on the fuel of desire for power, conflict and war are the inevitable results.

Nothing is stopping us from changing our ways and creating a new world, but we have invested too much in our beliefs and self-centred way of life simply to drop all conflicts and live in peace. We identify ourselves with the nation, the religion or the ethnic group we happen to belong to, and from this process of identification, conflict will automatically follow. We are all convinced that we are Americans, Britons, Chinese, Russians, Jews, Arabs, Muslims, Christians, Hindus, atheists and God knows what else. Identifying with such concepts is bound to lead to conflict, because the Jew and the Arab, the American and the Russian, or whoever else it might be, will tend to have opposing interests and demands, and all in the virtuous name of religion and so-called national security of course. There is no such thing as Christians or Muslims, Americans or Russians,

Democrats or Republicans, Socialists or Conservatives. All these are nothing but meaningless labels, and we are after all remarkably similar in our psychological make-up.

It is a widespread misunderstanding that peace is equivalent to absence of war, but it takes a lot more than that. Peace is an active, creative energy whose true source lies far beyond the human mind. It paves the way for an integrated and harmonious state of mind in tune with nature and the source of life itself. Peace in its true meaning will be a reality only when this state manifests in our own lives, which is only possible when the mind has fully aligned itself with universal consciousness as its true identity. Everybody who is still in conflict with themselves and their immediate surroundings will in one way or another inevitably contribute to keeping the wars of the world alive and well.

I don't really want to be harping on about this, but isn't it obvious that the human mind must have some kind of morbid fascination with conflict and war? We are constantly being bombarded with images and stories about war and conflict, and it has become so much a part of our culture that we seem unable even to imagine a world without it. It is as if we just can't get enough, as if we want to make sure that it is all perpetuated, and that we won't ever forget that this is how the world is, almost as if it has to be like this. A good example of this is how we constantly dwell on wars and armed conflicts of the past. To me this seems both bizarre and irrational, if not completely insane. People even put time and effort into re-enacting battles of the past, as if it is something to be proud of. And as if that wasn't enough, we also seem adamant in our efforts to preserve war sites and concentration camps, almost as if they are gifts from higher powers or something like that. I have to admit that I don't really understand what any of that is all about, and it makes absolutely no sense to me at all.

It would make a lot more sense to completely eradicate

from the face of the Earth all traces of concentration camps and other dubious memorials to our incredible bestiality, instead of making them into tourist attractions and something "we must never forget". We would do better if we gave these places back to nature, without ever coming close to them again, or at least not for a very long time. Only nature can heal the wounds created by the atrocities committed in such places. By insisting that we should never forget what happened, and saying that it must never happen again, we actually contribute to bringing the same tragedies about again and again. This is inevitable as long as humanity continues to be addicted to conflicts, violence, aggression and war.

The ugly truth is that many of us actually love violence, war, disasters, accidents and gory stuff, at least as long as we are not directly involved in any of it. Just look at all the rubbish that is being fed to us through the idiot-box usually known as television. It is absolutely incredible, isn't it? We even pay good money to watch movies in which people hurt, torture and kill each other. What pure, pristine and perfect insanity! How did it come to this? What in Heaven's name is wrong with us?

I suspect that most of us just want to continue to live in the same old way, battling our way through a seemingly endless series of problems and adversities. That is fair enough, but it is meaningless to ask why this world is full of war, conflicts, exploitation, corruption, poverty and misery as long as for all practical purposes we insist on being selfish, greedy, cunning, crafty, violent and fearful.

We may think that the problem is not so much that we are unwilling to live in peace and harmony, but rather that we don't know how we can accomplish it. That may be so, but it seems that very few of us are voluntarily going to let go of our entrenched materialist worldview and the selfishness and greed that go with it. The truth of the matter is that there is nothing stopping us from living in peace and harmony. Given the fact that peace, love and harmony are given to us in abundance by life itself and hence are immanent in each and every one of us, it is obvious that it must be far easier to live in harmony than in conflict. After all, generating conflict and war takes a lot of effort. Harmony, peace and love, on the other hand, are spontaneously present once we let go of our selfish, stupid and wicked ways.

For many of us it may still seem like a question of what we are to do to solve all the problems we are facing, but is it necessarily a question of doing something? Why do we insist on doing something all the time? Why can't we stop and just *be* for a change? Why is it so difficult for most people to be present to the miracle of life just as it is? Short of an inner revolution, we can't do much directly to change the world in more than just superficial ways anyway.

However, it is possible for every single one of us to change and thus embody a new kind of human being, and we can do this irrespective of age, gender, religious and social background or economic and political conditions. The point is that this is the only thing that can ever make any difference. Everything else is purely treatment of symptoms, which in itself is fine, apart from the fact that it doesn't really help much at all. A spiritual and psychological mutation is the only thing that can ever get to the root of the problem and thus forever remove the real source of the misery of this world. It is only when this has turned into a manifest reality that we will be living proof of a new humanity inhabiting a new Earth.

A world of harmony and cooperation

What would a new Earth of harmony and cooperation actually look and feel like, and is a world like that even possible? How would it all work in practical terms, and how would it be organised? Well, your guess is as good as mine, because at this stage we can only speculate, and speculation is ultimately pointless. Who knows how a peaceful, harmonious and sane world would be structured and organised, or if it's ever going to come about. The only thing we can say about that with any degree of certainty is that it would be very different from anything that anyone can presently imagine.

In spite of that, it is probably not entirely unreasonable to suggest that it would have to be much more decentralised than what is presently the case. Accelerating centralisation of power is the direct and unfortunate result of the insatiable lust for power and control that characterises the rampant and ruthless selfishness that presently dominates the world. An alternative to this is a world that might be organised along the lines of small, flexible, individual units and communities cooperating with each other, instead of the current nightmarish mix of globalisation, ruthless competition, faceless multinational corporations maximising profits regardless of consequences, rich countries exploiting the poor and so on.

A transformed humanity will obviously have to live in complete harmony with nature and all forms of life. The people inhabiting what we might call a new Earth would be working with nature and the environment. They would as a matter of course always be loving, honouring and respecting the natural world. Any agricultural activities would have to be conducted along the lines of what we today think of as small-scale organic farming and permaculture. Everything would necessarily have to be recycled and there would most definitely be no pollution and destruction whatsoever of the natural world. A sane humanity would have no use or need for fossil and nuclear fuels, but would find and develop natural and harmless ways of generating whatever energy they would need.

For most people all of this might seem utterly utopian, and in a way that's true because it is so far removed from almost everything we are presently experiencing that it seems almost impossible. Yet it shouldn't be too difficult to realise that any kind of destructive behaviour, whether it's on the individual or collective level, must necessarily be impossible for a humanity that is psychologically mature and spiritually awake. The new humanity inhabiting a new Earth would naturally and effortlessly be an integral part of nature and the environment quite simply because it would never even occur to them to see themselves as separate from any of it.

This new world will be peaceful, harmonious, yet also affluent. Human beings living in oneness and harmony will as a matter of course create a community, society and world free from conflict and selfishness. Humanity certainly has the potential for such a radical transformation, but there is no guarantee that it will ever happen. A transformed world can become a reality only through the spiritual transformation of the individual. For this to happen, authentic self-knowledge is absolutely essential. Each and every one of us has to realise our true nature as universal consciousness, the formless eternal that gives birth to all forms in all worlds.

In spite of all this, most people would probably think that a world of total harmony, universal cooperation and oneness sounds like a nice idea, but that it's all utterly unrealistic and utopian. However, in my view this is not such a far-fetched idea at all, but entirely realistic, and absolutely achievable by humanity. It won't come easy though, because the obstacles we are presently facing to make this a living reality are of such a nature that for most people they will seem impossible to overcome.

What exactly do I mean by a world of harmony, cooperation, unity and oneness? Quite simply a world in which all human endeavour, interaction and communication are totally free from conflict and based on everybody's shared values of love, integrity, honesty, compassion and kindness. Imagine what it would be like if everything in all areas of our lives was based on such values. What if the ways in which business, agriculture, medicine, environmental management, financial transactions, energy supplies and everything else were conducted from a universally shared vision of oneness and the living reality of the unity of all life?

The way things are at the moment seems very far removed from this idealistic vision of a peaceful Earth and all humanity living in complete harmony. The reason for that is of course that presently a majority of all human interaction arises from utterly selfish and ego-driven motives, which of course is bound to create misery and conflict. The point is that the ways in which almost everything is conducted must therefore necessarily lead to conflict instead of harmony, competition instead of cooperation and misery instead of fulfilment.

If we take a closer look at how a specific aspect of our activities as a species is played out, it might be easier to understand exactly how our ways of doing things often have such devastating consequences. You might not have given this a lot of thought before, or maybe you have, but just pause for a moment and consider how most of the ways in which we grow food and how agriculture is presently conducted lead to massive environmental degradation as well as having serious negative consequences for human health. The majority of agriculture is still based on using considerable amounts of artificial chemicals like pesticides, herbicides and fungicides, as well as artificial fertilisers, and it can be argued that the total impact of all this has never really been publicly acknowledged as the enormous problem it actually is.

The natural world does not know how to deal with synthetic chemicals so by using these we are essentially contributing to considerable soil depletion, environmental destruction and hence to our own downfall as a civilisation. Conventional agricultural practices have led to an alarming decimation of bees and other insects, which of course is having an ever-increasing catastrophic effect on all life, because it is all connected. In other words, if we cause harm and destruction to one area or one link in the natural world, all of nature will eventually suffer the consequences, and that does of course also include humanity.

All of this is driven entirely by selfish motives. As usual we are taking the easy way out by polluting nature even when doing something as basic and essential as growing food. It may seem like an easy and effective solution to spray poison on our crops to kill so-called predators, but the price we have to pay for that makes it in the long run a costly and inefficient way of farming. We may think that this kind of short-sighted and in the long run destructive behaviour is an acceptable compromise in an overpopulated world, but the simple fact is that it is creating more problems than it solves and cannot ever be brought into harmony with the environment and the natural world.

The only sensible way forward for humanity when it comes to agricultural practices is to start working with nature instead of waging war against it. This can only come about through a global switch to organic and small-scale farming methods, instead of massive industrial size agri-business models and genetically engineered crops.

Organic farming has seen a phenomenal increase in growth and organic produce are now more sought after than ever, and this seems likely to continue almost indefinitely. However, the organic sector is still a minority market, and in spite of having comparatively little negative impact on nature and wildlife, it is not yet big enough to effectively turn the tide. Conventional farming, often on an industrial scale, is still the dominating way of producing food, and as long as this is the case, agricultural practices will continue to have a destructive impact on the environment. This is the tragic reality of it, but we only have ourselves to thank for the long-term consequences. Anyone who is concerned about environmental destruction, and the widespread pollution of the natural world, must seriously consider switching to buying only organic products. If we still stick to non-organic, conventionally grown products, we will in effect contribute directly to the environmental destruction and harm we like to claim we are against. This means that environmental campaigners who are not actively supporting organic farming and buying organic products in their own daily life are being rather hypocritical, but hypocrisy is so common in our superficial and life-denying world that it's exactly what we might expect.

The thoughts on agricultural practices presented above are meant only as a concrete example of how we are digging our own grave through utterly selfish and short-sighted approaches to something that is so very basic to our health, well-being and ultimately to our survival. Nobody can deny or sensibly argue against the obvious fact that growing our food with the help of toxic chemicals, mega-sized agri-businesses and gene modification is an utterly selfish, destructive and ignorant way of treating nature and all life. We might think that the current state of affairs is all inevitable and how it has to be, but as long as we make convenience and short-term financial gain more important than anything else, nothing much is ever likely to change.

This kind of selfish behaviour repeats itself in virtually all other areas of human activity, with similar devastating consequences. We have to wake up to the fact that the problems facing humanity today have all been created as results of our utterly ignorant, stupid and ego-driven ways of conducting any kind of business or activity, not just agriculture. I used that as an example only because it might make it easier to see the connection between our lack of compassion for all life and the state of the world, but the same kind of story repeats itself over and over again in virtually everything we are engaged in as a species.

Any major kind of change seems unlikely in the short run, but we will sooner or later have to wake up to the reality of the mess we are creating, see the obvious connection to our selfish and ignorant ways, and hopefully change our ways to a life based on harmony, cooperation and love. That is our only hope of turning the tide so that we and all other forms of life on this planet can survive and prosper, and thus fulfil our highest potential.

Looking at life from a narrow-minded and self-centred point of view just won't do anymore, because it is precisely this attitude that has brought us to the sorry state we are in. It might all seem rather grim and hopeless, but on the other hand it is worth remembering that everything that's happening is in a sense necessary. Slowly, but surely, life is teaching us how to live in peace and harmony with each other, and regardless of how insane the world might appear to be, conflict, war and insanity cannot last forever. All things must pass, and sooner or later it is going to dawn on us that the source of all the world's problems and the solution to all our many difficulties reside within ourselves. When the majority of humanity finally discovers this and starts to live accordingly, we are going to witness a fundamental change to life on Earth of a magnitude that no one could ever have imagined. All of this is happening of its own accord, so there is no need to worry about what we should do to bring about whatever changes are necessary for humanity and planet Earth to survive.

Even if it is up to each and every one of us to live in a peaceful, creative and harmonious way, this whole process is in reality completely effortless. That might seem like a paradox, but never mind about that. Life often has a funny way of expressing itself through paradoxes, and there's nothing wrong with that. What is important though is that more and more people are beginning to realise that the responsibility for the state of the world rests with each and every one of us. Looking to others for solutions just won't do anymore. And what's more, there is no God or creator somewhere in some imaginary Heaven who decides what is happening to us and our lives. Each of us is in reality one with the source of life, and also a uniquely individual expression of universal consciousness, so we can't dump the responsibility on anyone else. That's the bottom line. No saviour will descend from the skies, or appear among us to make everything right. The only saviour who can ever make any real difference is immanent in each and every one of us.

The full realisation of your true identity as the pure, luminous presence of awareness is the key to a world without conflicts and wars; a world of peace, love, cooperation and harmony. That is the only sensible way forward for humanity and we have reached a point where authentic self-knowledge is no longer a luxury for the chosen few, but an urgent necessity for all of humanity. That is the key to humanity manifesting peace on Earth and a world filled with love, harmony and abundant creativity.

Free will and determinism

The discussion about free will versus everything being predetermined is as old as the hills, yet for the most part it has proved to be a complete waste of time. This kind of endless debating, arguing and pontificating can never really be resolved anyway, so when all is said and done, it doesn't seem to amount to much more than a lot of hot air. The mind can come up with all sorts of arguments and clever reasoning for both positions, but none if it will ever make any difference. That's because this kind of philosophical conundrum refers to something that doesn't actually exist, so therefore it cannot have a definite conclusion. It is a made-up and mind-based kind of problem, and has no existence outside of the realm of the mind and human thought.

It can of course be fascinating and mentally stimulating to try to come to a conclusion about such matters, but none of it will ever have the power to change anything on any but the most superficial level. We might perhaps adopt some new philosophical position in the process of pondering such issues, but that doesn't have the power to fulfil you or fundamentally change the way you live. Dreams and flights of fancy can be very exciting and even entertaining, but they have very little real impact, and philosophical musings fall into the same category in that sense. They can be endlessly fascinating, but don't have much substance and are soon forgotten.

It is of course entirely legitimate to enquire into this issue of free will, and if that is something you feel inclined to do, don't let anyone stop you. This kind of enquiry can and does have its own rewards and is not likely to do you any harm, so why not have a look at it. But what exactly is free will? Does it exist at all or is everything predetermined? Who or what decides what alternatives you seem to choose? Is it you, some kind of higher power, God or perhaps no one at all?

On the practical, everyday level you are the one that always decides what to do or not to do, or so it seems anyway. This is the common way of looking at it, but on the other hand, if we penetrate deeper into this matter, this seemingly innocent question is not that simple anymore. It is a prevalent notion that we are endowed with something known as free will, which implies that we make a choice after a process of more or less conscious deliberation. That is all very well, and all right as far as it goes, but there is more to consider than that.

If seen from the ordinary practical perspective, we may indeed have some kind of will, but it can hardly be called free. Most of us live a more or less mechanical life, based on ingrained habits, automatic reactions and instinctive impulses. It goes without saying that this has nothing to do with freedom, and that the choices we make consequently are rather haphazard and more often than not based on unconscious processes and inclinations.

You might be wondering who or what it is that makes choices, and that is indeed a very good question. We usually feel that we decide to do something, and by virtue of that are masters of our lives, but from where do these decisions arise? They arise quite spontaneously, don't they? Or do you decide to decide? No, you don't, because then you would have to decide to decide to decide and so on and on.

The point is that the choices we appear to be making really happen of their own accord, without anyone actually choosing or doing anything at all. It is life itself that in its many inscrutable ways spontaneously and naturally expresses itself the way it does. If we take credit for what is happening, we are deluding ourselves. Yes, there is a transcendent, omnipotent power governing everything, quite simply because this power is all that is. You may call it God, the Great Spirit, wholeness, universal consciousness, All That Is or whatever else you might fancy, because whatever words you use are just words and not the truth.

But if this is the case, you might be wondering how you can discriminate between what you think of as your own limited will and God's will. Well, that's actually not very difficult, because God's will is literally identical with what exists in this moment. What happens here and now is God's will. Everything that exists is this will, and it's got nothing to do with our ideas about making choices and decisions. This higher form of will is identical with the all-embracing presence that is expressing itself as all the different forms of life. God's will truly is free, so in that sense you could say that there really is something called free will, but it doesn't spring forth from the human mind and all its limited and limiting activities.

In other words, we could say that we have free will to the extent that we have moved beyond the mind and a limited egocentric identity, and recognised our true nature as pure awareness, but other than that, we don't actually have free will. We only appear to have free will, and the beautiful paradox and sublime irony in this is that in spite of our lack of actual free will in the traditional sense of understanding it, we are still compelled to act as if we really do have what we usually think of as free will. Because of this we might as well just accept as fact that we do have free will, even if that so-called will is not strictly personal or owned by the limited ego identity we usually think and feel that we are. Most of human interaction and our moral values are based on this notion of each individual being in possession of what we think of as free will, so in that sense it is not something that we can just sweep under the rug and then pretend that it doesn't exist. While it may be true that we have to act as if we have free will, actually we don't, or at least not in sense we tend to think of it.

We usually think that there is a little me somewhere inside our heads that chooses this, that or the other, but that is all an illusion, and free will in this sense doesn't exist. On the other hand, absolute freedom is a reality, but it is not within the realm of the human mind. Freedom is part of the nature of universal consciousness, so it's nothing personal in other words. In that sense, free will is a reality, but don't make the mistake of thinking that you can ever take personal possession of it, because that would be nothing more than the ultimate expression of self-deception.

As for the question of whether everything is predetermined or not, this problem is nothing but a loosely woven mental cobweb without any substance at all. This kind of philosophical exercise is quite irrelevant, and only makes sense within the limited confines of the human mind. To think that anything is predetermined hardly has any relevance in the context of practical day-to-day living, or as a tool for navigating our way through the maze of daily life, and as a philosophy of life it's a claustrophobic dead end street.

Nothing is prior to the endless expanse of this moment, and everything arises spontaneously and effortlessly here and now. We can think and speak of the past as real on a purely practical level, and that's entirely appropriate and useful in that context, but the reality is that the eternity of now comprises everything. Past and future are the inventions of the human mind. They are ideas or mental experiences that can arise only now. When you take a closer look at all this, you realise that no concepts, notions or ideas have any real content. We have to use words in order to communicate verbally, but in the ultimate sense only the consciousness that you are is real.

Philosophy, theology and suchlike might all be very interesting and entertaining, but when you look into it, you realise that the whole lot of it is just about as substantial as the twittering of birds, but not nearly as beautiful. Through thousands of years philosophers, pundits and theologians have thought, speculated, contemplated and pondered to no end, but what has ultimately come of it all? Not very much apart from an endless supply of thoughts and ideas, theories and guesswork, sometimes in the form of grand and impressive philosophical edifices, but when all is said and done, isn't it all just "much ado about nothing"? The simple fact is that no thought or idea, no matter how deep and seemingly profound it is, can ever express truth. Even if philosophers more often than not are great thinkers, that doesn't count for much when it comes to realising the truth of who you are and what life is. Thought can never grasp the ultimate truth of life, and moreover has a tendency to complicate everything, often creating problems where there are none at all.

An excellent example of this is the so-called problem of evil, which essentially concerns itself with how evil can exist in the world if God is good and loving. After all, if he's such a champion chap, how come he would even have considered creating this miserable world and filled it with such horror, deceit, evil and pain?

The so-called problem of evil doesn't actually exist, because there is no God as a person who created the world sometime very long ago. Neither does long ago exist other than as a concept, but what is more important in this context is that our ideas of good and evil are nothing but mental fluff empty of true meaning. We are constantly stealing fruits from the tree of knowledge about good and evil, and we are obviously finding it very hard to realise that all ideas of good and evil are nothing but totally subjective values. We are always talking about something being good or bad as a consequence of how it affects us and what we can get out of it. It is always the mind that defines what is positive and negative, but no such concepts can have meaning, value or content in an absolute and objective sense. Only Life itself exists, and its grandeur, majesty and ultimate reality are so totally beyond any of our limited ideas of good and evil that such concepts ultimately must be regarded as meaningless.

More often than not, we like to keep ourselves busily engaged in trying to shape life according to our own narrow-minded concepts of how it ought to be, and according to what we think is best for ourselves. The inevitable result of this activity is all the struggle, conflict and controversy the world is so full of. Most people would argue that much of what is going on in this troubled old world is wrong, bad and utterly lamentable, but all such assertions are just opinions and amount to nothing more than chewing the mental cud. In the final analysis, if ever there is one, all our fanciful and clever opinions are worth diddly-squat, regardless of how smart and elegant they might sound.

It is common to think that some things are bad and wrong and that they should be different from what they are, but our incessant attempts at improving the world only seem to make it worse, and moreover prove that we think we know better than life does. It is tantamount to saying that life doesn't know what it's doing, as if we are thinking, "well, if I were in charge and ran the universe, then everything would be so much better..." and so on. Life always knows best, and everything is exactly the way it is, so why waste time trying to argue with what is? What is happening is always right in the absolute sense, quite simply by virtue of the fact that it is. I know very well that it doesn't always seem or feel right, but that's only because we are unable to see the totality of life. The problem is that we usually see everything from the narrow and confused perspective of self-interest and selfishness, but none of us can improve or change what life is giving us, because nothing can be different from what it is. Change is obviously always taking place, but that's nothing that we need to take credit for, because it's just life itself singing its song and dancing its dance.

Yet on the other hand, on a purely practical level, it certainly does seem as if we can change and improve conditions and circumstances. We can imagine different alternatives and make adjustments according to these, and there is nothing wrong with that. In actual fact though, there are quite simply no possibilities other than the one life happens to present to us right now. This also includes all our ideas about different options. If you imagine an alternative to what is happening now, then that thought exists in this moment, and you just can't change it. All thoughts, actions and whatever else you think is going on are happening spontaneously, right now. Nobody is doing anything. Things happen, just like that, for no particular reason, or at least not for any reason that the human mind can easily relate to or understand.

This moment, what is here and now, seems so fulfilling and complete in itself that it is hard to understand why anyone would ever want to get to the next one anyway. Well, there isn't a next one, so it is a futile effort and an avoidance of what is. There is of course never any need to try and escape from what is, because there's nowhere else to go. And regardless of what life presents to us in the unfathomable eternity of now, it is all a mystery of such grand and multidimensional proportions that it is completely beyond anything we can ever hope to understand. Why make up a story about a non-existent next moment when the only real moment is so endlessly fascinating? Even what we tend to think of as ordinary day-to-day stuff is really something utterly extraordinary, and we can easily realise that if only we let go of our preconceived notions and ideas about it.

There are no ordinary moments, only this eternal mystery here and now. Nothing can really be said about it. We can only merge with it and be this mystery. The totality of existence is nothing but the supreme universal intelligence of All That Is, mysteriously and creatively expressing itself as what we know as Life.

All is well throughout existence, and all is part of a higher harmony in which nothing can ever be out of alignment. It is of no particular importance whether we say that everything is predetermined or a result of free will, or if we think that there really is a problem of evil that we must somehow solve. Whether we think it is all dream or reality, or if we define something as a fantasy and something else as real is of no importance. The only thing that is important is that no matter what you experience, whether it is a dream, your ordinary so-called reality or anything else, the pure light of awareness that you are is the crucial foundation for all of it.

You are the conscious awareness which is the witness to and source of it all. Everything comes and goes, appears and disappears in what you are, and no matter what is happening, you are unquestionably here and now as indestructible and unchangeable presence. It doesn't matter at all whether the world is illusory or real. Only consciousness, awareness, being, or whatever word you want to use, is ultimately real, and everything else is just the stuff that dreams are made of, coming and going in a process of incessant abundance and creativity. Only awareness exists in an absolute sense, because awareness is beyond form and therefore eternally indestructible and unchangeable.

Universal consciousness is the one true reality; that which always abides. That is what you are. You can't doubt your own existence. Your very being is beyond time and space, untouched by birth and death, forever indestructible. What appears and disappears is only like a dream within the true reality of what you are, and can't ultimately be called real. It is only that which exists by virtue of itself that is real, and untouched by all appearances on the level of form. Only universal consciousness, which is what we truly are, fulfils that condition. Awareness *is*. Everything else is more or less dubious, debatable and somewhat contentious, and the question of whether we have free will or if everything is predetermined is essentially of no importance and has no real practical value. Unless we approach philosophical riddles like that with a playful attitude, and unless we see the absurdity of it all, we would all be better off forgetting all about such matters. A much more enjoyable and fruitful approach is to just live and love life as it is. Love is the answer, all is well and the harmony of all life forever rules supreme.

Karma and reincarnation

One of the most popular ideas in spiritual circles is the concept of reincarnation, and by extension also the concept of karma. Much has been said and written about this subject over literally thousands of years, but all too often such talk tends to become little more than idle speculation, if not pure nonsense. It might all be a lot of sound and fury about absolutely nothing at all, but it really depends on your point of view. I want to assure you that I am certainly not claiming to have anything new and revolutionary to contribute when discussing this subject, but even so, I think there is a way of looking at this which at least to me makes quite a bit of sense within the philosophy of the oneness of all life.

Most of us tend to think of ourselves as separate entities living our lives in a material world that exists independently of consciousness itself. Even if some of us sometimes try to imagine what life might be like in some kind of heavenly realm, we still have a tendency to think of such a realm as a world that exists independently of consciousness. This deeply held belief in being a separate entity living in an objectively real world, whether that world is a material or a non-material one, makes it difficult for us to understand the true nature of life and thus also understand how reincarnation and karma might work. We are fundamentally expressions of the divinity of life itself throughout our wondrous voyage between birth and death and beyond, yet at the same time it would appear that all our thoughts, words and deeds are crucial as to what direction life is taking at any given time.

So even though it may seem as if we are separate entities incarnating again and again in different bodies across aeons of time, and there is plenty of circumstantial evidence to suggest that this is the case, it is closer to truth to say that there is only ever the one universal consciousness expressing itself through all its different forms. From this perspective, there is neither time nor reincarnation, but only the incessantly unfolding creativity of life itself. We are in reality one with the immense creativity that is the essence of everything, and all of life is one.

Our actions, thoughts and words play an important part in creating the reality of what we think of as our life, because everything is intimately interconnected in the oneness of life. While there seems to be a great deal of truth in that, everything is still nothing but the spontaneous expression of the one universal consciousness. There are no separate entities doing anything. Life is all-inclusive and omnipresent, spontaneously unfolding and forever taking on different forms in a display of creativity that is way beyond anything we can ever hope to understand. And yet, in spite of that being the case, it is perfectly valid to say that every act has its repercussions, and that sooner or later we shall have to face what we have set into motion.

I seem to recall that once upon a time I came across a book in which it was claimed that we reap tenfold of what we sow. That's a pretty good way of putting it, and if that is the case then everything is indeed recorded in the great book of life, which would mean that we can't get away with anything. So if what is reflected back to us from the world around us is a kind of projection of our internal landscapes, the world can be seen as an externalised representation of what we ourselves have created through our thoughts, words, emotions and actions.

The most common way of explaining karma is to say that it is purely a simple system of cause and effect. This would suggest that everything is decided beforehand, based on our previous actions, thoughts and so on, but in reality there isn't anything like beforehand. There doesn't actually exist anything previous to what is. The notions of previous and later may have practical value, but aren't of much use to describe reality.

While it certainly is true that whatever we do has its

consequences, the structure of the mind and the way it has been conditioned right from birth tend to make us experience everything within a time frame. The time interval is an illusion, but we won't be able to see that until we move beyond the limited domain of the mind. All actions, consequences, causes and effects exist within a timeless reality, and are being played out on the infinite stage that is all of life and existence.

The main reason we tend to entangle ourselves in misconceptions about reincarnation has to do with our subjective sense of time. As already mentioned, our idea of time is just that: an idea. It is an invention of the human mind, and for that reason we tend to see the question of reincarnation within the framework of time. To the extent that we choose to believe in continuous rebirth, we automatically think that one life follows another, just as one day seems to follow the next. However, this is a misguided conclusion, precisely because we live in a timeless reality, regardless of whether we are aware of it or not.

Because we tend to think of time as a linear process, with one moment neatly following another ad infinitum, our ideas about reincarnation are skewed and greatly distorted. Reincarnation, as understood according to this view of time, is therefore a rather misleading concept. We can, however, recognise reincarnation as being a fundamental aspect of life itself, but only in the context of seeing it as a natural process that completely transcends our notions of existing as separate entities within a framework of sequential time. So in this more factual understanding of reincarnation, it is in reality just another expression of life itself, another modulation of the conscious oneness that is all. There aren't actually any separate and fixed entities or souls jumping from one physical body to the next, and while that may certainly appear to be the case, it's just another one of life's many fascinating paradoxes.

So what is it that reincarnates if there isn't a separate self, soul or entity that can do that? Every form that has ever existed is totally unique, never to be repeated, so every one of us has our own unique flavour and characteristics. We all have specific physical, emotional, mental and psychological tendencies and traits, and while these are all unique to the individual form, they do not belong to a separate ego or entity as such. All of these tendencies live on as an imprint in the cosmic web of life and are inherited by other life forms at some point in what we think of as past, present or future. You may incarnate into a different life form or forms, but what you are in essence is always and forever exactly the same, namely universal consciousness, which is all there ever is. What you usually think of as your personality traits, peculiarities and talents may be inherited by some other person somewhere else in what appears to be another time and place, but that person is not you in the way that you think of yourself now. None of this is of any great importance, but in any case it may be a good idea to spare a thought for the life form who is inheriting the fruits of whatever you are manifesting in this reality.

While there may well be some truth to this admittedly awkward and superficial explanation of how reincarnation might work, what is much more important than any such explanations is that what you really are is the pure luminous presence of awareness. This light of pure being was never born and will never die, because it isn't just another entity in the endlessly fascinating world of forms, but rather the formless eternal reality in which all forms are born, live and die.

In a sense, all ideas and theories about reincarnation are redundant, and maybe even irrelevant. Universal consciousness or awareness, which is your true identity, exists outside of time and space, or you could say it is the formless and primordial emptiness of being. This is the origin and also the very essence of body, mind and psyche, and indeed the fundamental reality of all existence. Even though it may be convenient to say that you are born into physical existence time and time again as a particular person and then die after some time, this is really nothing more than a highly simplified verbal translation of something that can't really be explained in words. You could even say that all incarnations exist simultaneously, but even that is just another concept that doesn't really explain anything very well at all.

What you are is a lot less than what you think and it is also a lot more. It might sound like some kind of paradox, but it is not too far off the mark to say that you are nothing and everything at the same time, that your eternal being is beyond time and space, and that whatever concepts we might use to describe any of this are meaningless. What you have come to know through God only knows how many incarnations of life in physical form is only like a fleeting shadow compared to the multidimensional miracle that is the totality of life. Life on Earth is more like a dream than anything else, and although this particular kind of dream might seem both very important and real to us, it will soon enough pass away and be forgotten.

Even though absolute truth is a living reality, no thought or idea can ever fully express that truth. That is really the long and short of it. As long as we use words to try and understand or explain any of this, it is all bound to appear rather contradictory and confusing. The problem is that because mind is an instrument ideally suited to operate within the dimensions of time and space, it finds it difficult to grasp the timeless and formless reality that is beyond all thoughts and mental concepts. It is quite correct to say that ultimately neither time nor reincarnation has any valid existence, but all the same it is useful to speak as if these concepts refer to reality. To use reincarnation as an example, we could say that this is only an explanatory model we can use to get a better mental grasp of life on Earth, which we experience as a real phenomenon in time and space.

All this may seem to imply that time and reincarnation are facts of life, and in a certain sense they are, but you must always keep in mind that anything to do with time and space is only relatively real, if we can put it that way. What we are, our spiritual essence, experiences what appears to be a physical world in time and space, seemingly repeating the experience time and time again, across centuries and millennia. This whole process is an adventure to be enjoyed, so taking it too seriously is never a good idea.

Life is a gift, an exciting and playful affair, and we're best off enjoying it to the best of our ability. The pain that the world is so full of is the inevitable result of our boundless selfishness and greed, and of our insistence on seeing ourselves as separate entities in an objectively existing external and fundamentally material world. Still, even this is part of life's sparkling fireworks. It is our ignorance and lack of insight into the true nature of life and its infinite modes of expression that make it difficult to understand that everything that's happening is just life itself continuously celebrating the joy of creative expression. Life is an inscrutable mystery, and the dimension in which there is time no longer can only be realised right now. Now's the timeless, and nothing more can or need to be said about that.

Please do also keep in mind that if you should happen to come across someone who is suffering, it may be that the suffering person's karma is to receive help from you, and it may be your karma to help him or her. You know nothing about that, and you can't do much else than follow your heart's calling anyway. That's really the bottom line, not whether there is karma and reincarnation or not. When all is said and done, that is nothing but speculation and philosophy anyway, so there is no need to bother with it, unless you are philosophically or speculatively inclined of course.

What you do or don't do in any given situation is ultimately not that important. What you are is where the rubber meets the road, and if you have realised the truth of what you are, right action will much more easily follow. It's not really possible to express the nature of your true identity in words, but for the purposes of this discussion it is near enough to say that you don't exist as a separate entity, that you are the great nothing expressing itself as you, and as everything else for that matter. Once you get your identity sorted out, you will also see that everything is interconnected, part of the same indivisible reality, in time as well as in space.

The only thing that is of any real importance is what you are, and no teaching can ever reveal that to you. It is something you can find only through your own experience and by creating your own path as you travel it, no matter where it might lead you. Whether there is reincarnation or not is ultimately irrelevant, so maybe it's best to forget about such trivia. The journey of life in the eternal now and infinite here is its own destination, and its essence is that of unconditional love.

Love

What is love? There are many ways of answering that simple question, and the most straightforward response I can come up with is that love is the innermost essence and very heartbeat of all life. For that reason alone, love is much more important than anything else in life. Without love, whatever we do is bound to create conflict, and is certain to fail. It is love that gives meaning, value and purpose to our lives. It has been said that it is only when the power of love is greater than the love of power that the world will know peace, and as far as I know, that is true. It logically follows that love is what will ultimately bring about peace on Earth, and without unconditional love flowering in our hearts we will never see the day when peace on Earth is a living reality. So love is not something that can be neatly tucked away as just another aspect of our lives. If it is to have any meaning at all, love has to embrace the totality of your life, because if it doesn't, then all ideas and concepts about love are nothing but empty and meaningless words.

Love doesn't know any compromise and isn't something that's up for negotiation. What we usually think of as love works within limitations and certain conditions. It is easy enough to say "I love you" to somebody, but unless that love is unconditional, it's not really love at all, and will have a tendency to be present only as long as the other person meets one's expectations and helps to fulfil one's desires. The moment the object of one's love looks at somebody else, or does a bit more than just looking for that matter, love tends to disappear rather quickly. Then jealousy, suspicion, demands, self-pity, hate and sometimes even violence tend to emerge. I have often heard people say that such reactions prove one's love, but ridiculous statements like that are made from a state of ignorance, not from wisdom.

What we usually think of as love relationships are

unfortunately more often than not tainted by power struggles, possessiveness, jealousy, demands, pressure, mutual gratification and exploitation plus various other forms of conflict. These are perhaps experiences most of us have been through in the name of love, and it's not without reason that so many people think that love is often a source of conflict. But how can love ever be the source of conflict? That just doesn't make any sense.

People even use the expression unhappy love, but can love ever be unhappy? No, that doesn't make much sense either. Love can of course never bring unhappiness, and neither can it be the source of conflict, aggression or hostility. Where there is love, there can be no conflict and unhappiness. It is just like darkness and light; they can't coexist. Darkness is nothing but absence of light, just as conflicts, hate, evil, fear, jealousy and suchlike are nothing but the absence of love. Let love flower, and all misery will vanish in the twinkling of an eye.

The beauty, excitement and fulfilment we experience when a mutual attraction develops between two people, to the point of falling in love, is of course a truly magnificent and wonderful gift. But maybe we should call that experience rising in love instead, because that is in fact much closer to its true nature. After all, love is the most natural expression of who we truly are, hence rising in love is such a sweet, lovely and fulfilling experience. What actually happens when we are blessed in this way is that the identification with the centre, the little me or ego is temporarily broken, or at least greatly diminished. The sweet, loving, beautiful and innocent beings that we fundamentally are come to the fore, and are expressed much more directly than what is usually the case. This is why we experience being in love as something truly exceptional, which it certainly is.

The experience of rising in love is also an open invitation from the wholeness of life to expand, grow and flower together, and is very fertile ground for realising and fulfilling our true potential. It is in the context of a romantic love relationship that we have the greatest chance to truly go beyond the illusory ego that most of us tend to identify with most of the time. It is an opportunity to literally create love, and the act of making love and engaging in sexual union is especially important in this respect. Making love is so much more than just a bit of fun and pleasure now and again; it is a sacred union, and can in fact be a most exquisite portal into ever greater fulfilment and the realisation of the divinity of all life.

For most of us, though, the initial euphoria of love doesn't tend to last. When identification with the false ego identity starts building again, conflicts in various forms will to some extent also start to reappear. It is very rare for couples to be permanently in love for more than a few months at the most, but why shouldn't this state of pure, innocent, sweet and exciting love be present as a vital and nourishing power and a permanent quality of our most intimate relationships? However, for that to happen, a high degree of presence, compassion and understanding, as well as unconditional love, must also be present. Consequently, being in love and creating, manifesting and making love as a natural way of life depends to a great extent on whether one is psychologically mature, spiritually awake and innocent enough to let love flow freely, come what may.

Most of us will have experienced this kind of innocent and pure love straight from the source from time to time, but this kind of experience is usually tied to a certain person, a place or some other particular aspect of one's life. In order for these feelings and experiences to manifest, we often seem to depend on something or somebody else, perceived as being outside of ourselves. But genuine love is all-embracing and limitless. If it is truly flowering, it includes everything and everybody, and as such it is unconditional and unqualified. Love must necessarily include all. If you truly love somebody, that love surely must include everybody and everything else as well. Then you love even the few people you might not like that much, as well as whatever life might happen to bring to your doorstep. Nothing is excluded from true love; it includes all living beings, as well as the Earth, the sky and the universe.

Even though what we usually think of as a love relationship may be the most fertile ground for being a channel for unconditional love, entering such a relationship with fixed ideas of what it should be like will more often than not lead to problems. If we do that, we set ourselves up for trouble, because all love relationships are dynamic and spontaneous expressions of life itself and will not conform to anyone's preconceptions.

Any ideas you might have about monogamy, polygamy or even celibacy for that matter are totally meaningless in the face of love. If you try and live your life according to any particular formula you are bound to end up in some kind of trouble, because life will always throw a spanner in the works in some way or another. Just be open to what manifests now, because that is the only reality you will ever know. Anything else is just a story you make up in your head, and that story is bound to make you suffer, because it is more often than not in conflict with what is. This may come across as a rather radical kind of love, but let's dare to be radical for a change. Let's abandon all ideas of right and wrong and just live life to the full, come what may. That seems like a much better way of going about things than what usually goes on in the name of so-called love relationships.

Love effortlessly embraces everybody and everything. Once you let go of your habitual reactions and demands, you also allow a new world of love and true passion to emerge. You may then experience a kind of compassion for all life that you had never known was possible. This is a way of relating to life that has nothing to do with desire, sentimentality and emotional reactions. It implies a far greater sensitivity to the plight of all living beings, and is the only authentic and natural way of life.

A pattern of reactions is always something that's a result of conditioning, and is more or less automatic, whereas a heartfelt response is always spontaneous, honest and natural. To some it may seem like a paradox, but love is distinguished by an infinite depth of feeling while at the same time being free from emotional reactions.

Nobody can do anything directly to make the miracle of love happen. It is of such a nature that I don't think it could ever yield to any kind of method or be caught by any formula. The only thing you can do is to be open and receptive to it. Yes, you can certainly open your window to the enchanted garden of love, but you can't force its delightful fragrance to enter your house.

Luckily, there is no recipe for learning how to love. If there had been a method or technique for learning the most beautiful of all arts, then love would have been worthless. A method implies that you practise something to reach a predetermined goal, one that has been more or less clearly defined beforehand, but love can never be a goal in that sense.

There is no way to learn to love, because love itself is the way. Love is always new, unpredictable and creative, and can never be caught by thought and the mind. It is only when we let go of our attempts at finding or owning love that it has a chance to blossom. That is when the flame of love burns brightly. This energy belongs to the wholeness of life, so it is neither yours nor mine. It is the origin of everything, and nobody has the power to control it or bend it according to their own wishes. Love is almighty, can do anything, and it is what will ultimately change the world and finally create peace on Earth. Who knows why we are here on this Earth, but it wouldn't come amiss to live in unconditional love no matter what gifts life bestows upon us. That is as good a life purpose as you are ever likely to get.

Love never comes and goes; it is always here now. Love transcends everything, because love is completely beyond time and space, yet the miracle of life is such that love is somehow made manifest in this dream reality we think of as the world. Love is what I am, what you are, what we all are. Love is by far the most important thing in life, and everything else is just details. We do the best we can of course to get the details of life and existence right, and to get things working the best we can, but at the end of the day, it doesn't really matter that much whether we experience success or failure, affluence or poverty, pleasure or pain, life or death. Our ability to manifest, express and share love is what ultimately decides the quality of our lives.

To manifest and share unconditional love is the greatest gift we can ever give to anyone. Love is also the only thing that can truly make a difference in the world, the only thing that can change this mad, tragic, dysfunctional and self-obsessed world for the better. Love depends on nothing else and is owned by nobody. It cannot be quantified or made into a commodity. It is just too vast, wild and powerful for anything like that. Love is the only thing in the world that is ultimately real, but then it's not a thing and it's not of this world. It is the transcendent reality of what we are.

Death is the greatest illusion

In terms of trying to figure out what life might have in store for us, the only thing we can ever know with certainty is that we are all going to die. For every single one of us there comes a time when we have not only departed from this world, but when not even a single trace or memory is left behind to show that we have ever walked this Earth. Death is the great equaliser. It shows us clearly that in essence we are all the same. Death makes no exceptions and thoroughly annihilates everything and everybody. So we try to cope as best we can by inventing all sorts of philosophical systems and religious beliefs, all in order to avoid facing the bottomless void of our own existence and the fact that we are all sentenced to death.

While it certainly is true that life as we usually think of it is a temporary affair, it is also equally true that we are not the one who is dying. The body, mind, psyche, various energetic bodies, plus whatever else we might think we are made of, are all temporary manifestations of universal consciousness. Everything appears to be in a constant process of being transformed into something else, but you are separate from all that, yet at the same time it is all an expression of what you are as eternal consciousness.

Even though death is not negotiable, nothing can touch what you truly are. What you are is not of this world and is beyond all form. Your true being cannot die, because it was never born and is beyond time and space. What you are in essence exists by virtue of itself and doesn't depend on anything else. You are everything and nothing, the infinite emptiness that is the ultimate fullness. Our true nature of formless consciousness is the source of everything that can ever be known on the level of form. It is the foundation for all of life's different manifestations, and also its many forms and individual expressions. This paradox can't be rationally explained, and that is part of the great beauty of it.

Whatever adventures we are involved in are nothing but dreamlike dramas enacted upon the great stage of life. The fact remains that it is only what you are that is ultimately real, yet that contains all experience within itself. Life on Earth is a dream, the astral plane is a dream, heaven is a dream, hell is a dream, time is a dream, space is a dream, matter is a dream and the whole history of humanity and the universe is a dream. The dream might be experienced as real, but it is real only by virtue of being yet more manifestations of formless, all-inclusive consciousness.

The story of your life, your personality and everything else that goes with it will be eradicated sooner or later and vanish as if it had never existed anyway. It goes without saying that what doesn't last is ultimately illusory. That which abides is the only thing in the world that is real, but then, it is not really a thing, and it is not really of this world. You are that.

There is no death. You are immortal. You were never born and death cannot touch the essence of who you are. Yet it is equally important to remember that whatever you seem to be on the level of form is finite, mortal and temporary. This might appear to be paradoxical, contradictory and confusing, but that's all right. Life itself is a big paradox, at least as long as we are trying to understand it intellectually, and as far as what happens when we die is concerned, we'll all find out soon enough anyway.

Most people have a rather neurotic and fearful relationship to death, but this is completely unnecessary and based on ignorance and lack of self-knowledge. Trying to avoid death seems both natural and futile at the same time. There is an inbuilt impulse for survival within us, yet at the same time there is absolutely no way we can ever outsmart death, or at least not in the long run. Death is never going to let you down, so thank your lucky stars for that.

We would rather not know anything about death, hence it has become taboo, something we don't even want to acknowledge the existence of, unless it is absolutely necessary. Sweeping the Grim Reaper under the rug doesn't help at all of course, because that venerable old gentleman is always going to pop up again, perhaps even with a vengeance. The simple truth of it is that if you want to get rid of death, you must get rid of birth, because everything that exists on the level of form is temporary and all things must pass. Life and death are in reality two aspects of the same process. It is all a great and glorious drama in which we all have a golden opportunity to discover the truth of who we are, and the absolute certainty of death can be a great help in this respect.

In spite of all that, it is of course also appropriate to acknowledge that it is always a sad time whenever someone close to us dies, or when we otherwise come face to face with death. The emotions that tend to arise in such circumstances are entirely natural and should be fully accepted and expressed in whatever way that feels true to you. On the other hand, it is also important to realise that death is not only an occasion for mourning, but also a stark reminder that life in this world is transitory and impermanent. It is nothing but a brief sojourn through the rather strange kind of reality we usually think of as life on Earth.

Death has the potential to make us aware of the eternal without which nothing of what we think of as life and the universe could ever exist. Nobody ever dies; our true nature, what we really are, has no real home in the dimensions of time and space. The essence of what we are has its abode in the dimension of eternity and cannot ever be touched by what we think of as death.

Death is not so much an end as a transition, and it does perhaps make us think about what is truly important in life. It is said that you can't take anything with you when you leave this world, and while that may be true as far as the things of this world are concerned, there is nonetheless something that will always remain with us, through life, death and beyond. This is our capacity to love. To the extent that we have mastered the art of love, we could say that we have lived a successful life, regardless of what we may otherwise have accomplished on our journey through this world.

The capacity for unconditional love is still a relatively rare gift in our world, but if there is one thing that this world needs, it is love. Not the love that depends on anything or anybody else, but a love that transcends everything and exists by virtue of itself. Our greatest challenge in life is to embody this unconditional and selfless love, and as far as I'm concerned, it's the only thing that is of any real and lasting importance. To the extent that we have made unconditional love a reality in our lives, we have not only given the most precious gift to our nearest and dearest, but also greatly enriched humanity and the world.

The overwhelming majority of people are motivated primarily by fear and greed, which is what is making this world into the madhouse it presently is. Making love a reality in our lives is an absolute necessity if we want to create a better and more peaceful world. Peace on Earth can become a reality only through a complete transformation of human consciousness. Authentic spiritual transformation quite simply means that greed is transformed into generosity and fear into love.

Why are we afraid of death? Isn't it because we cling to an imaginary identity, a separate ego-self that is constantly struggling to assert itself and gain security for itself? The greed and fear that are so prevalent these days, and have been ruling humanity for at least the last few thousand years, are nothing but expressions of selfishness. They are the results of being conditioned into believing that we are separate entities that somehow need to fight with each other and struggle for power in order to survive. The selfish notion that we have to get as much as possible for ourselves, even if it is at the expense of others, is really based in a deep-rooted fear of death, of not existing as a separate entity.

This is a very unfortunate misunderstanding, because this fear is totally baseless. One's notion of separateness is an illusion, just as our idea of time is an illusion. We usually think of life as having duration in time and extension in space, but these are just tricks the mind plays upon itself in order to make some kind of sense of the mystery of life. Life is conscious, creative, intelligent awareness of an order and magnitude that is beyond what we can presently grasp, even though this awareness is precisely what we truly are. We are not separate entities at all; we are life itself.

The vast majority of people believe that when they die, they will either go to heaven or to hell, or just cease to exist. However, we need not really concern ourselves with the question of whether or not there is life after death, because if we look more closely at this, we will come to understand that we exist in the dimension of eternity and that all concepts about before and after are quite meaningless. There is no death; there is only life, which is consciousness, being and love. Whether we live short or long lives is at the end of the day of no great importance, because whatever we think our life is, it hardly amounts to more than a swiftly fleeting dream in universal consciousness. What we think of as life, the universe and everything are all part of the divine play of consciousness externalised on the level of form, yet always abiding and resting in and as itself, beyond form, time and space.

Nothing in this world matters that much, or at least we could say that nothing matters absolutely. The realisation of this simple fact does not mean that you become callous, cynical and insensitive. Quite the contrary, you play the beautiful game of life to the best of your ability, delighting in all its many facets.

expressions and seasons. You realise that your greatest gift is that of unconditional love because that is the one thing in this world that truly transcends everything. That is because love is not really a thing of this world. Love is the formless, unnameable divine expressing itself through the world of name and form. It is the divine made human. It is God incarnate on Earth.

Creation is now

A lot has been thought, said and written on the subject of whether enlightenment, spiritual awakening, truth realisation or whatever you want to call it is a result of one's own effort or if it is all down to grace, divine or otherwise. But does it really matter? How important is it to find an answer to such questions? I don't know if it is of much importance, but I do feel that if we are to understand any of this and come to any kind of conclusion that makes sense, it is vital to understand that the personal self is ultimately an illusion. From that perspective there isn't really anyone there to make an effort in the first place. There may be the appearance of effort being made and personal will being exercised, but in truth there is only ever the one expressing itself as the many. You could even say that there is grace even in what we think about as effort, and a kind of divine effort manifesting itself through what we see as grace.

Ultimately effort and grace are one, and once you get a feel for that, the question of whether one should make an effort or leave it all to grace falls away as irrelevant. It is only the false ego-identity temporarily created by fragmentary thinking that struggles with such questions. Spirit is unconcerned with such labels and definitions. Walk whatever path you feel drawn to, practise whatever feels true to you and other than that just leave the rest to life itself.

The underlying assumptions in the discussion about effort and grace are that we are separate entities existing and going through a process of development within a time continuum and that salvation may be at hand sometime in the future. This is a discussion that can never be resolved as long as these assumptions are not questioned and scrutinised. This kind of debate can exist only as long as we believe that we are separate entities living in a world that exists independently of consciousness, and that there really is such a thing as time.

It is almost universally accepted that time in the sense of linear motion from past through present into the future is a reality. Religious and atheist believers, scientists and philosophers, political talking heads and ideological demagogues, spiritual seekers and virtually everybody else all subscribe to this notion. This notion of time is something that we all tend to take for granted, even though there seems to be a great deal of confusion and disagreement about what time actually is.

Time certainly seems to be a real phenomenon, and it is obviously a concept that we all have to accept, at least on a purely practical day-to-day level. If we didn't, life as we know it, in the kind of civilisation that we are part of, would be next to impossible. However, that doesn't mean that we can't question this idea and try to explore whether it's a given fact of life or if it's nothing more than a practical convenience to make life easier to navigate.

What if time is essentially a fantasy or illusion that the human mind has cooked up? Regardless of its practical function, time is fundamentally a concept that continually must be created and maintained, and as with all mental constructs, it has no more reality to it than a flimsy daydream. This fantasy we call time is part of the dream that humanity is dreaming. It can even be seen as being an essential part of the dream, because without the concept of time, we would find it much more difficult to keep playing the game of life in the way that we have become accustomed to. What we think of as time is nothing but a dream arising within the human mind, like a giant octopus rising up to the surface from the murky depths of the collective unconscious, entangling everything with its sticky tentacles. Whatever is seen through the lens of time tends to be perceived as dim and distorted, and true understanding thus becomes less likely to manifest and express itself.

It is easy enough to see that the eternity of now is all there ever is, but only when it is clearly understood that this is quite literally the case, will the idea of time start to lose its grip on the mind. The idea of living in the now is very popular among spiritual seekers, and has always been so, but I do get the impression that most of the people who advocate living in the now are still fanning the flames of past and future, as if the present is the best option of the three.

In order to grasp the illusory nature of time, it is very helpful to realise that creation isn't an event that for some inexplicable reason happened in a more or less distant past. Creation is constantly manifesting and spontaneously unfolding as this inscrutable spectacle we think of as life, the universe and everything. Time must continuously and actively be created by the mind to have any semblance of reality. All stories of creation and cosmology are nothing but elaborate fantasies created in the eternal now and it really doesn't matter whether we believe some God character created the world sometime in the good old days or we believe that the universe sprang to life billions of years ago in some kind of gigantic cosmic thwack and developed from there onwards. Regardless of which model we subscribe to, they invariably depend on the idea of time to make any sense at all. The only problem is that time doesn't exist as an objective and independent phenomenon. It is a dream, a fantasy, magically and spontaneously manifested in the eternal now.

Eternity is now and all evidence of past, or future for that matter, effortlessly springs to life in the eternal now. The scientific and religious models of creation are similar in the sense that they depend on time to exist and make sense. They miraculously spring to life in this moment, just as the writing of these words and the reading of them do. Creation didn't happen in the past. All creation is now, this is it and we are it. The universal consciousness, being, presence that is all is incessantly manifesting and expressing itself in this way. It is spontaneously and joyously celebrating itself. It doesn't need time, because it is all that is, and all this is that.

The creative power of life itself is beautifully and elegantly manifesting and unfolding the entire life span of that nobody in particular that you think of as yourself. It is as if consciousness is painting a picture on a vast canvas, effortlessly creating you and what you think of as the entirety of your life. That all of your life story – past, present and future – spontaneously is being created and is springing to life now might understandably seem like an illogical and unacceptable idea. However, if you let this idea sink in, and play around with it for a bit, you might eventually come to see the whole idea of time, evolution and ultimate destiny in a very different light.

A shift in perspective is necessary to see through the illusion of time, in fact you could say that this amounts to nothing less than a paradigm shift, because it shatters the very foundation of how we think life works. Once you see that time as we usually think of it literally has no independent and actual existence, a heavy burden falls away. It is as if life takes flight, allowing you to gracefully surrender to the eternally unfolding mystery of all that is.

So to get back to where I started, and in light of the above, it is clear that it doesn't really matter whether enlightenment is a result of effort or grace. Regardless of what form one's spiritual search and awakening may take, it is all unfolding quite spontaneously in the eternal now. We might think that at least to some extent we have the power and ability to influence life and evolution, but in actual fact, nobody is ever doing anything and everything is just happening, because that is how the supreme intelligence of life is spontaneously unfolding.

One could say that everything is grace or that everything is due to whatever effort we make, but all such statements are ultimately meaningless. Life itself sometimes takes the form of effort and sometimes of grace, but it is all still just this one miraculous manifestation from somewhere far beyond the world of form. This will be much easier to see and appreciate if you let go of the notion that you are a certain somebody doing something or other to reach somewhere in the fullness of time. Then you might even realise that you are nothing but life itself dreaming that it is you, just like it is dreaming that it is me, or anyone or anything else. In other words, there is no need to take anything personally.

Working on yourself and focusing on your spiritual life in order to become enlightened is perfectly fine, regardless of what form it takes. In fact, I would go so far as to say that whatever you are doing at this time to work on your spiritual development is exactly the right thing, because that is what you are actually doing, and this is how life expresses itself through what you think of as yourself.

There is nothing that in and of itself is written in stone or indispensable in this dream of life and living. As long as you remember to be kind and loving to all living beings, live lightly and consciously, you will inevitably make a positive difference to the world and help to create a new Earth. Be a light unto yourself, and never look for or desire rewards, recognition or praise, because ultimately they are all worthless. Love is its own reward. Sharing your love with the world and everybody you meet is the only true benediction, and the greatest gift you could ever give to anyone.

As for spiritual practice and enlightenment, there is no only way that everybody somehow has to follow. We are all the same universal consciousness expressing itself in ever new ways. We can never really go anywhere else than the infinity of here and it can never be any other time than the eternity of now. Creation is now and this is it.

Beyond spirituality

Life is a funny kind of business, and there are of course a multitude of opinions and theories about what the ultimate purpose and meaning of it might be. There are many ways of relating to life; you might look at it as an incomprehensible mystery, a precious gift from a divine source, an exciting and rollicking journey of pain, pleasure, tragedy and comedy, the ultimate form of absurd theatre, or maybe as an endlessly fascinating journey going ever deeper into the most beguiling enigma, like a strange kind of multidimensional and seemingly unresolvable puzzle. You may go even further than that, and adopt the utterly illogical and ridiculous philosophy of reductionist materialism and think of life as nothing more than a blind, unconscious and mechanical process of haphazard events leading to nothing more than a pitiful, pointless and ultimately futile end. But regardless of how we see life, it would appear that most of us spend the majority of our lives chasing after some kind of fulfilment or satisfaction, but often sacrificing the glorious miracle of the eternally present in order to reach some kind of goal in an imaginary future.

How we see life and deal with its many challenges can and will vary quite considerably, but regardless of how we go about it, do we truly know what life is? We might think we do and we might have all sorts of theories, beliefs and bits of information about life, but when it really comes down to it, isn't it obvious that we don't really know much at all? Nobody knows anything, apart from the obvious fact of being alive, and the impermanence of everything that appears on the level of form. In other words, we are simultaneously conscious of being and of our physical mortality.

In spite of our actual ignorance, we all seem utterly convinced that our own particular beliefs, methods and systems for the development and improvement of self and society are superior to all others. Even in those cases where the practices and underlying philosophy of these beliefs are utterly absurd, otherwise seemingly intelligent people seem to hit a blind spot when it comes to their religious or spiritual beliefs and practices.

It is all due to conditioning of course; if we are told repeatedly from the moment we are born that something is true and that certain things need to be done and other things need to be avoided if we are to achieve eternal salvation, then most of us tend to believe it, regardless of how ludicrous it might be. All major religions and the majority of New Age philosophies and alternative spiritual traditions have their fair share of this kind of turbo-charged twaddle. All the same, most believers and practitioners will happily go about their business convinced that salvation shall be theirs, if not in this lifetime, then certainly either at death or in some imagined future existence, whether it is an earthly or a heavenly one.

Most of us tend to live our lives thinking that we know who we are and what we need to do to find fulfilment or salvation. The fact that so very few of us ever seem to find anything like salvation or peace of mind doesn't seem to make much difference. Every religion, sect or faith, including many New Age groups and other contemporary expressions of spirituality, sell something that they don't actually have. They make the same promises in one form or another, and there are always plenty of customers who are willing and ready to buy into a bit of cleverly presented deception. It is fairly easy to see through the illusions presented by organised religion, but how many of us can see that the same game is being played out in most of the systems presented to us in the guise of more up-to-date forms of spirituality?

People who consider themselves trailblazers of the spiritual world and right at the cutting edge of human development don't tend to go for the salvation presented by outdated systems like Christianity, Islam, Judaism and Hinduism. These days the grand prize is known as enlightenment, but for the most part it is just the same old stale wine in new and sparkling bottles. It is obvious that for most spiritual seekers, enlightenment is nothing more than an idea of a perfect state or type of experience that is the ultimate fulfilment, a kind of cosmic orgasm that is everlasting and always on tap. With this comes the notion that once one has reached this ultimate state of perfect divinity, all one's problems disappear and one is like a light to the world, worshipped and looked up to by everybody else.

Behind these ludicrous ideas lies one fundamental assumption that is hardly ever questioned by anybody; namely that one exists as a separate entity, a soul or something similar, and that this entity, this me, will sooner or later attain enlightenment, at least if the right type and amount of effort is put in over a long enough period of time. In other words, typical New Age spiritual people have a great desire for enlightenment, but want to be enlightened as they are. That is asking the impossible, because as long as you still carry this idea of being a particular somebody who can attain a certain everlasting state of bliss or benediction in the fullness of time, enlightenment is nothing more than a fantasy, an illusion, a dream. It might be a very beguiling and beautiful dream, but it's a dream all the same. For most spiritual folk, enlightenment is thought of as something within the realm of experience, some kind of supremely satisfying state, as something that can be attained, regardless of how arduous the task may be and how many lifetimes it might take to get there.

Most religions, sects and spiritual groups promise eternal salvation in the future, whether they call it enlightenment, nirvana, moksha, liberation, Kingdom of Heaven or whatever, but only if you follow their prescriptions, and quite often the reward is to be collected only at the time of death or in some future life or existence. Part and parcel of this belief system is also the idea that for those who don't follow the only approved way, punishment is at hand in the form of eternal torture in hell, rebirth into suffering almost without end or other dubious scenarios of an unpleasant nature. They are playing on fear and greed in other words. The promise of fulfilment is something to be attained in the future, through whatever methods of purification and self-development that are prescribed, but only as long as you don't stray from the straight and narrow. This kind of approach is one that is likely to keep people in bondage, fast asleep and blind to the truth of what they are and what life is.

What so very few seem to grasp is that anything within the realm of experience is temporary, nothing more than a fleeting glimpse, the stuff that dreams are made from. Regardless of what form one's experience takes, the one fundamental question remains: Who is the experiencer? What is it that is aware of these words and their meaning? What is it that gives light and life to all experience? All experience seems to take place within the dimensions of time and space, yet the awareness that is the all-accepting, non-judging witness to all experience is itself completely beyond time and space.

Awareness is what we are. It has no existence on the level of form, regardless of whether form is seen as external or internal. This is our true nature. It is nothing, yet everything; nowhere, yet everywhere. All is contained within it. Without it, all levels of experience, from the most material and dense to the most subtle, refined, heavenly and exalted, indeed the whole universe, all forms big and small, would have no existence, reality or validity whatsoever.

From the point of view of consciousness or awareness, all experience is of exactly the same value and equally valid. In other words, whether you are enjoying aeons of the most exalted and blissful states of Samadhi or you are lying face down in the gutter on a cold and rainy night, blind drunk and sick as a dog, choking on your own vomit, it's fundamentally all the same. You are there as the witness of it all, as consciousness, regardless of what form the experience takes. It is all experience, therefore transitory, and hence something that sooner or later will come to an end. All things must pass, even Nirvikalpa Samadhi and all her other friends, whatever they might be called, must sooner or later depart. Regardless of what all the religious pundits, New Age gurus and latest hot shots in the spiritual marketplace might say, there is no state that is everlasting. There is no salvation in time. There is no enlightenment that will provide you with everlasting bliss. There is nothing that will save you from yourself.

What religion or spiritual path do you need apart from life itself? What's the point of going to religious services in churches, temples and mosques other than to be brainwashed into ever deeper states of sleep? Isn't life in all its mystery and unfathomable glory enough? The gift of life is always here now, but if you always hanker for fulfilment in some imaginary future, you'll miss it, and you won't be able to know yourself or what life is. This great adventure is always available, ready and waiting, even in the seemingly most mundane and tedious. In fact, if you stop and let yourself melt into the wonder of the eternal now, you'll see that there isn't anything that actually is mundane or tedious. Then you'll know that life is not something that you own or have; it is what you are. The universal consciousness that is your true being is never born and never dies. It is beyond time and space, yet embraces all time and space. When this is fully realised, this eternal now of life and love reveals itself as the gift and blessing it truly is.

Many of us toil and struggle for years and decades to attain spiritual enlightenment, freedom, liberation, Samadhi or whatever else we like to call it, but the irony of it all is that the little me, the ego, the person, can never become enlightened. It is only when consciousness wakes up from the dream of ego and separate identity that freedom blossoms, but then there is no longer anyone there to attain anything. There is only the ease of being nobody in particular, accepting and enjoying life as it is.

Many people seem to think that spiritual awakening necessarily has to be some kind of ultra-cosmic spectacular event, but this is not the case at all. All experiences are just experiences, regardless of how profound and cosmic they might be. All experiences are really the same in one sense, whether they're so-called mundane and common or whether they're experiences of mystical union and enlightenment. The common denominator in all is what you are, the vast nothing that is everything at the same time. That is neither an experience nor a state. It is totally beyond even the most profound spiritual experiences and mystical states.

There is nothing wrong with taking on a persona or an ego identity because life in this world would be difficult or at the least somewhat impractical without it. Whenever it is called for, the ego is perfectly all right, but only as long as you are not identified with it. As long as you know that your true nature is that of universal consciousness, of awareness itself, the ego is not a problem. This is what makes the big difference, not whether you have cosmic experiences of mystical union or not.

You may of course still occasionally experience discontent about certain things being as they are, or have the experience of certain needs not being met. On the other hand, there is the peace and contentment of being and consciousness. These seeming opposites appear to be coexisting, but they're not really opposites, because consciousness contains all, accepts all, welcomes all and is indeed all. Nothing outside of consciousness exists and all forms are yet ever new modulations of consciousness. In other words, the discontent is just like ripples of the surface of a mighty, endless ocean of infinite possibilities. There is nothing than needs to happen for truth to be realised. Truth already is. It is this consciousness, presence, being, awareness that you are; this nothing that is everything.

The beauty of spiritual awakening is that it happens quite spontaneously. Nobody can plan or in any way force an inner flowering of this nature. This miracle is possible only when you are ready for it, which is whenever you are innocent enough to surrender to life as it is. We are all unique expressions of formless consciousness. That is what is waking up, or perhaps it is more accurate to say that consciousness is waking up from the dream of separateness and ego. This miraculous inner flowering will forever remain a great mystery, and I doubt that it can ever be fully explained.

Enlightenment is nothing but the knowledge that I am whole, complete, limitless, ordinary, all-accepting awareness. Every living being shares the same essential identity, and all is one. All forms of life are in constant flux, always changing, appearing and disappearing. The only constant is awareness itself, which neither changes nor disappears. All is revealed in the light of awareness. Nothing can ever disturb or affect awareness, hence its nature is that of peace, love and happiness. This is what we all are, and ultimate fulfilment is possible only in the full realisation of this simple fact. Nothing else will do, and it is freely available to us all in the glory of the eternal presence of now, just as we are, and regardless of what the circumstances of life may be. That is the supreme irony of life and also its greatest benediction.

Freedom from boredom

Why is boredom so prevalent in the modern world? Why do a lot of us get so easily bored? You would have thought that with all the entertainment, activities, information and technology available to people in the modern world, it would be almost impossible to feel bored. But in spite of all that, if you scratch the surface of our modern self-satisfied lives a little bit, it is easy to see that boredom is now endemic in our civilisation. It is right there underneath all the sound and fury, glitz and glamour, success and affluence. All our ceaseless activity, our many gadgets and gizmos, the abuse of alcohol, prescription medication and illegal drugs, an endless supply of mind-numbing entertainment, politics, religion and all the rest of it, provide plenty of evidence that we are on a seemingly endless mission to escape from ourselves. It's almost as if the vast majority of us would rather not look at the true reality of our sorry, shallow lives and the chaotic and miserable world we have created.

The fact that we are so easily bored says a lot about where we're at; basically, we are going nowhere fast, and with all the latest technology and gadgets to show for it. But without knowing who we are and what is ultimately most important in life, it is all rather meaningless. It doesn't matter how many people, things, activities, gadgets and whatever else we fill our lives with. As long as we are still desperately fighting to cover up or run away from the bottomless void we might occasionally just about sense somewhere within, our superficial lives are only going to continue along their present trajectory towards a pointless and pitiful end.

If you consider the absolutely inexplicable miracle of existence itself, if you contemplate the astonishing fact that there is something rather than nothing, if you reflect on the incredible gift of consciousness, indeed if you consider life itself in all its miraculous glory, then how can you ever be bored? It is only possible to be bored if you have cut yourself off from all this and taken the make-believe falsity of what we know as life in the modern world as a substitute for life itself. This is what it's come to; our whole way of life has turned into nothing but a substitute for real, authentic, passionate living.

It is no coincidence that virtual reality, transhumanism and artificial intelligence are now some of the hottest topics around. This seems to be the direction in which the majority of us are heading, and we are travelling down that road mostly because of relentless indoctrination and our increasing addiction to technological wizardry. A sophisticated global technocracy will do nothing but enslave us and gradually turn us all into cyborgs, totally incapable of empathy, critical thinking and true intelligence. The dystopian reality of that kind of brave new world will never save us from ourselves or help us overcome our many challenges. It certainly won't bring peace, prosperity and creative flowering, but most of us seem totally oblivious to the fact that we don't really need any of this high-tech nonsense. It's all just part of a gigantic experiment of creating yet another invisible prison for ourselves, and if left to continue, it will ultimately lead to humanity making itself redundant. It's really just a pathetic and unnecessary replacement exercise for directly experiencing our unbreakable bond with nature and Mother Earth, thus consciously embodying the living truth that we are all unique expressions of.

Our civilisation is usually considered the most advanced that has ever existed on the face of this Earth, but that begs the question: What exactly do we mean by advanced? Most people would probably think of this in terms of our technological prowess, and that's fair enough, but how can technology in itself be a sign of development if we insist on using it in the service of death and destruction? We might seem technologically advanced compared to just about any previous civilisation that we have any kind of knowledge of, but isn't it rather obvious that we are also very primitive in so many ways?

The last 150 years or so have seen a drastic and unprecedented development in technology, and even though many aspects of human life have improved considerably during this time, it's also been by far the bloodiest, most violent and destructive period in all of known human history. We speak about peace, but practise war. We have high ideals about generosity and altruism, but worship at the altar of greed and selfishness. We like to think we are compassionate and loving, but aren't we more often than not controlled and motivated by fear?

When we look at the world around us, it might be easy to descend into a deep dark hole of despair, because the human condition and indeed our civilisation seem so chaotic and difficult, so utterly full of conflict, pain and misery. There are of course many promising and uplifting signs of more and more people waking up and choosing love instead of fear and generosity over greed, yet at the present time, so much of what we are doing in all areas of life is to a very large extent life-denying, negative and based on selfishness. We can see this clearly displayed everywhere; just look at what is happening in politics, law, health care, agriculture, education, religion and just about everywhere else. The following quote, attributed to Michael Ellner, sums it up quite succinctly: "*Just look at us! Everything is backwards, everything is upside down; Doctors destroy health, lawyers destroy justice, universities destroy knowledge, governments destroy freedom, major media destroy information and religions destroy spirituality.*"

In our insane and irrational world, stupidity is considered a virtue, ignorance is hailed as wisdom and shallowness is seen as profundity. Very few people seem to have the courage and intelligence to just stop and question the lies, ready-made conclusions and stupefying brainwashing we have all been exposed to virtually since the day we arrived in this world. How many of us truly have the courage and intelligence to question all answers?

It is obviously a lot easier just to accept what you are told, instead of looking beyond the superficial and delve deeply into the unfolding miracle of life. Most varieties of our modern media, especially television and the movie industry, have become nothing more than tools for indoctrination and putting its consumers to sleep. The mindless blathering that is presented as news in our culture hardly ever amounts to more than cheap entertainment, brainwashing and propaganda. It is a very successful tool of hypnosis that has been developed to create a manufactured kind of reality where even the most bizarre events and statements are swallowed and digested by the news consumers without questioning or further scrutiny.

It doesn't take much to see that most of us live in a make-believe world, and through example teach our children to do exactly the same. Sooner rather than later a make-believe world is going to appear very boring indeed. In spite of all our affluence, success and technological progress, we are fundamentally getting only more superficial, selfish and stupid every day.

We've now reached the point where the most likely long-term outcome is a full-scale implosion and a painful end to our entire civilisation. In such a scenario things would get very real very fast, and that would be the end of boredom forever. It doesn't necessarily have to play out like that of course, but because we insist on clinging to our false personas and unnatural way of life, our selfishness and stupidity, it may well be what we are heading towards.

So what is the alternative to the escapism that is so prevalent that it is considered quite normal? How can we break free from the insanity that has become so ubiquitous that it is seen as sanity? What about facing up to what we are, the kind of lives we are living, and the superficial values and blatant excesses of our civilisation? If we could only do that, and let go of our false notions about ourselves and the world, a dimension of freedom beyond anything we could ever have imagined would start to open up for us. All that is needed is for each individual to wake up and realise the nature of his or her true identity. But is that likely to happen anytime soon? Aren't we all just too busy trying to escape from ourselves, and defend our attempts at self-deception to death rather than facing the simple truth of what we are?

What is freedom anyway? On the most basic level, it means the power or right to act, speak, or think as we want as long as no harm is done to anybody else. We can also think of it in terms of political and social freedom, which is increasingly being eroded and encroached upon across the world, but freedom is a lot more than that. It is an inner dimension that's without borders or limitations. It is essentially liberation from the illusion of a limited self. Freedom in this sense of the word is not something that is separate from you; rather it is the very essence of what you are. You don't have to do anything to achieve it, because you are it. On the other hand, it is perfectly fine to do whatever you are already doing because freedom is still intrinsic to your true nature.

When all is said and done, does any of this really matter? One could convincingly argue that it doesn't make a lot cf difference what does or doesn't happen, and that whatever we might think and say about any of it hasn't got much power to change anything at all. After all, this life and existence, indeed the whole wondrous universe and whatever else that appears on the level of form is no more than a multifaceted, kaleidoscopic and endlessly fascinating kind of cosmic multimedia show spontaneously arising in universal consciousness. Whatever seems to be happening on the level of form and personality may thus not be all that important after all. It is a play, a divine dance in which the forces of creation, maintenance and destruction balance each other out and ultimately are seen to be one and the same. It is nothing less than celestial harmony in action.

However, in spite of all that having a great deal of truth to it, on our journey through life, within the context of our day-to-day escapades and adventures, it is not always so easy to see that all is indeed well throughout the totality of creation. Trouble, conflicts, suffering and despair seem to be everywhere these days, and it's often difficult to know how to cope with it and what to do about it. Be that as it may, because as long as you put unconditional love, kindness and selflessness first, you will have attained a degree of freedom and enlightenment that no adversity or human selfishness can ever touch. Love is its own fulfilment and reward, and your daily personal life is the stage upon which it must be fully realised and expressed. And if you can see the truth of that and live up to it, you will also have said goodbye to boredom once and for all.

Nobody's enlightenment

There are many different spiritual paths and many types of spiritual seekers, but most of them share one fundamental characteristic: the concept of enlightenment and the importance of becoming enlightened. For the most part, enlightenment is thought of as some kind of rarefied state of all-pervading eternal bliss and peace, in which one is supremely detached from all worldly and personal concerns. Throughout history a wide variety of paths and spiritual practices have been devised, developed and perfected in the pursuit of this most exalted of all states. The many different paths and schools of spirituality may be in conflict with one another on many issues, but they do tend to agree on at least one thing; namely the supreme importance of consistent and committed practice under the guidance of a spiritual teacher over a period of years, if not decades or even lifetimes to even start approaching the final goal of spiritual enlightenment.

So the question is: Do you need to make an effort to attain enlightenment or is it already a done deal? The first thing we need to realise when trying to answer this question is that both approaches to enlightenment and spirituality are very attractive to the ego. Some egos love the idea of making great effort over a long period of time in order eventually to achieve the great prize of enlightenment. On the other hand, a different type of ego feels attracted by the idea of already being enlightened. Enlightenment is supposed to be the ultimate reward, so when you are told it is already the case, why would you even bother to make an effort? Never mind the fact that many people who adopt the idea of effortless enlightenment already being the case are still as miserable as sin, but if you can somehow convince yourself that you're already enlightened, what does it matter?

Regardless of what most spiritual seekers might claim, they

still tend to operate within a paradigm in which there is a state of enlightenment to be achieved, whether or not one makes an effort to get there. Because of this, enlightenment is often just yet another goal, something else that is the object of a seeker's desire. It is probably no exaggeration to say that most people in the world desire money, power or some degree of material luxury, whereas a sizeable minority desire the eternal bliss and peace that allegedly are the hallmarks of spiritual enlightenment. The latter may come across as more worthwhile and noble than the former, but it is all still desire. Your desire might have been sublimated to some degree if you are a spiritual seeker, but that doesn't change the fact that desire is still desire regardless of what form it takes.

Enlightenment is usually seen as some kind of superhuman, elevated, special state, and the ego likes to keep it that way. The ego always likes to be special, and that holds true not only for the worldly ego but also for the spiritual one. It is of course possible and maybe even a worthwhile pursuit to reach elevated states of profound bliss and peace and to have all sorts of spiritual experiences along those lines. However, all experiences and all states are really nothing but temporary events that appear and disappear within the all-inclusive reality of pure consciousness. This holds true even for the most exalted spiritual experiences and the most sublime states of mind.

The endless discussion concerning which spiritual path is the best, most effective or the most elevated one is nothing but a manifestation of ego wanting to be top dog. Everybody is convinced that his or her particular path, practice, group, guru or teaching is the best and highest, and that everybody else is engaged in more or less mediocre practices. Such is the nature of the ego; the desire to be special, to be best and the most highly advanced. In actual fact, all paths and practices are merely life expressing itself in yet more inimitable ways, none of them in essence any better or worse than any other. We are all unique expressions of this one life that is all.

Enlightenment does not and cannot exist within the realm of time and space. Enlightenment has no existence in the world of phenomena and form. Whether we traverse the physical, mental, psychic, astral or any other realm, we will not find or attain enlightenment in any of them. As long as we see ourselves merely as separate individuals existing in a material world of time and space, or even a spiritual world for that matter, we are likely to be chasing experiences and personal fulfilment in one form or another. The worldly man seeks fulfilment through the world of the senses while the spiritual seeker is chasing the projected fulfilment of enlightenment. Worldly desires may be fulfilled, at least temporarily, but the desire for enlightenment cannot ever be fulfilled, except as a delusional fantasy, because enlightenment doesn't exist within the dimension in which desire operates. The individual, the seeker, the spiritual aspirant will never know it, and the idea that we have already arrived at enlightenment is as mistaken as the idea that we can ever get there.

Enlightenment cannot be achieved by the person, the individual, the separate entity, the ego. It can flower only when the seeker, the meditator, the ego, realises that a strictly personal identity is a fictitious one, and that his or her true nature is that of universal, limitless consciousness. This is not necessarily some exalted or exceptional and rare state, but rather that very same consciousness that is aware of these words and their meaning, because that is the only consciousness there ever is It is all-pervading, always present, completely non-judgemental and totally accepting of all and everything. It is the effortless unfolding of life itself and all its forms, yet doesn't depend on anything outside of itself, because it truly is all there ever is and ever can be. In other words, life and all its forms absolutely depend on consciousness because consciousness is what they are all ultimately made from.

Consciousness itself depends on nothing, because it is all that is and also totally beyond all that is. It is beyond all words, teachings, experiences and states yet includes everything within itself. Universal, limitless, totally ordinary consciousness is your true nature, and once you realise this, all talk of spiritual development, awakening and enlightenment becomes completely superfluous. Then you are happy just to be what you are and go with the flow of life wherever it takes you.

Being what you are is totally effortless and enough unto itself. There is nothing to add to it, and nothing to take away. The secret of enlightenment is revealed not by striving, but by relaxing, not by amassing more knowledge and spiritual credentials, but by totally letting go. Just let go of who you think you are, go with the natural flow of life and all will be well.

What you are looking for is what is looking

The search for truth and enlightenment can quite rightly be called the eternal quest, yet the irony of the spiritual search is that it is the seeking itself that is the final obstacle to realising your true nature. The truth of what we are is always freely available here now, but we always think it is elsewhere and invariably look to the future for fulfilment. This is absurd, because what we are looking for is what is looking.

What, then, is the reality of our true nature? Trying to put the truth of what we are into words is not at all easy, but it is not too far off the mark to say that universal, eternal, limitless consciousness is our true nature. I know that statements to this effect have already been presented numerous times throughout this book, but it is still worth repeating that there is only ever the one universal consciousness expressing itself as the innumerable forms of what we think of as life.

Maybe you still think that this seems like a rather strange, paradoxical or illogical thing to say, and that's fair enough, so nothing wrong with that. So if, after having read this book, you still find statements about universal consciousness being your true nature to be strange, silly, incomprehensible or unacceptable, that's perfectly all right. Nobody needs to agree with any of this, and it certainly isn't yet another belief system. It is something that anyone can immediately and easily see for themselves. You can effortlessly see the truth of this in your own experience.

This alternative view of reality is not one that fits well with what is generally accepted as true, real and factual. It is most certainly starkly at odds with the mainstream materialist worldview that most people take for granted these days, and just cannot be reconciled with such a limited and primitive philosophy of life. Once you have seen through the illusion of what you have come to think of as your "self" and left behind any investment in maintaining and developing a story about "me and my life", it no longer matters so much what happens or what people say or think about you, or about anything else for that matter. When you live from this understanding there is an undercurrent of subtle joy silently accompanying everything you do and there is a quiet compassion for everything and everybody, even those few people you might not like that much.

Now that is all very well, but how does this relate to the world around us with all its problems and conflicts? Most of us will agree that the world is in a very sorry state, and that it doesn't seem to be getting any better. There is no shortage of conflicts, wars, poverty, misery and suffering. Most people will probably also say that this sad situation can best be rectified by more or less drastic changes of a social and political nature. Put a different system in place, improve social conditions, replace a few politicians with some others, make distribution of wealth and resources more fair and balanced, introduce better legislation, encourage more international talks and treaties between nations and ethnic and religious groups and so on and on.

There is of course a place for all this, and there is nothing wrong with any of it, but the question is: Can any of it really lead to making the world a better and more harmonious place? I maintain that in the long run it cannot, quite simply because the core reasons for the wretched state of the world are not to be found in things being organised in an imperfect way. The germ of it all lies buried deep within us, and as long as it isn't dealt with on that level, no real and lasting change on the outer level is possible. Isn't it obvious that it is at the core level changes will have to take place if anything in the world is going to change at all?

Many of us also feel that we have to do something to try and make the world a better place, and this in itself is a noble and beautiful response to the chaos and suffering humanity has created for itself. However, if we want to improve society and change the world, it is really a question of where the intention for doing that comes from. If it comes from a state of anger, vanity, selfishness, greed or narrow-minded righteousness, then any action undertaken will only perpetuate the present state of affairs and do little more than add fuel to the fire. It is the quality of consciousness manifesting through each individual that is the deciding factor in all this, and any action undertaken from a state of love, peace, harmony, understanding and freedom will most certainly have a positive impact on the world. In other words, for the world to change, the individual must change. The root cause of all conflict, misery, war and disharmony in the world is precisely the very mistaken idea and feeling that, "I am a separate individual, living in a world that exists independently from me, and therefore I have to fight and struggle to get what I want and to survive." Our whole civilisation is built on this idea and it is very much a part of what is making the world into the madhouse it currently is.

It's hardly news to point out that the world as we know it today is predominantly being run by greed and fear. These two very basic forces seem to be the drive behind most of what the majority of us do. Isn't it obvious that for the world to change into a better place, fear will have to be transformed into love and greed into generosity? We can continue and try to change the world as much as we like, but as long as it is done from a blinkered place of ignorance of one's true nature, then nothing is likely to change at all. However, it's easy enough to say that love needs to replace fear and generosity needs to replace greed if the world is to change, but that is not going to be very helpful or even meaningful if we fail to understand where greed and fear come from.

Right from the day we are born we are being conditioned into conforming to the culture and worldview of the society in which we find ourselves. A newborn baby is like a clean slate, completely innocent, full of wonder and without even the slightest idea of self and ego. A little baby is also like a sponge, eagerly soaking up whatever attitudes, beliefs and behavioural patterns it is confronted with. In many ways this is inevitable and maybe even necessary, but it is as if most of us never really grow up and reach true human adulthood. Most people are nothing but traumatised children in more or less old bodies, mechanically acting out unconscious patterns and reactions, engrained in them since childhood.

We live in a world that is pretty much totally insane, but in a sane world, childhood would be left behind when entering into adolescence. That is of course almost impossible for a young person as long as virtually all its adult role models are nothing but children themselves. The full realisation of one's true nature ought to be a natural stage of development and really just a matter of course during one's late teenage years, but this is so rare that it is almost unheard of in the kind of world we have created.

The realisation of one's true nature simply means realising that one's persona, one's role in the world and one's whole history is nothing but a mask and a story, at best a kind of functional entity, and that in truth there is no self or true identity on this level. All appearances to the contrary, there is no personal, individual, limited self enclosed inside each of us. There is only limitless and timeless universal consciousness, presence, awareness, spirit, being, and it is within consciousness itself that the brain, body, world and universe are all spontaneously arising. We are all expressions of the one being that is all and also completely beyond it all. It is only because we generally are so ignorant about this simple fact, that there can ever be any conflict, war or misery at all.

Once our true nature wakes up from the dream of ego and separation, we also realise that it really doesn't matter that much what happens, because we know deep down that all is well. This world is nothing more than a dream anyway, but we don't have to make the dream into a nightmare, which is what we are presently doing. We can live creatively in this weird, wild and wonderful world and make it into a beautiful place, filled with love, harmony and peace. What is needed for this to happen is nothing less than an inner revolution, a radical transformation of the human psyche. It necessarily implies discovering one's true nature; the realisation that we are not separate, that we are all unique expressions of the one Great Spirit that is all. This is the deep inner knowing that the formless consciousness we are is the essence of everything and ultimately what the world is made from. Only the authentic realisation of what you are can change the world, because only then will unconditional love flow freely. Only then will we live in true abundance, which quite simply means that our love effortlessly shines with equal compassion on all.

The recognition of oneself as universal consciousness is the one thing that will bring about true change for the better in the world. As long as the vast majority of humanity is still adamant on being selfish, greedy, fearful and ignorant of their true nature, the world is never going to change. We can't have it both ways. We can't hold on to our selfishness and ideas of I, me, mine, and also have peace on Earth.

But is spiritual transformation on a global scale likely to happen anytime soon? As far as I can see, it doesn't seem to be imminent, but the truth of the matter is that nobody knows, and nobody can know. Anyone who offers predictions along those lines is talking nonsense. Despite a lot of talk in various spiritual circles about how more and more people are waking up these days, I have to admit that in spite of my best efforts, I struggle to see that this is the case for the vast majority of humanity.

In spite of this I do know that all is well, that within the wider context of all that is, nothing is out of balance. Everything is in perfect harmony, and we would do well to remember that life is far too mysterious, inscrutable and multidimensional for any of us to truly know its ways. Let's allow life to express itself freely through us. Let's celebrate the miracle of love and of being alive. Life is the answer just the way it is right now, and you are the answer just the way you are right now. And regardless of how difficult our situation as a species may seem, it is always possible that one fine day the greatest miracle of all may indeed become a living reality for all.

Returning to the Garden

The mythical paradise often referred to as The Garden of Eden is a concept that has always been with us in some form or other. Somewhere deep down in humanity's psyche the dream of returning to the Garden has always lingered on. We are probably all carrying this longing within us, whether we are consciously aware of it or not. Yes, certainly, a planet governed by love and harmony sounds lovely, but is that even possible? Is there really any chance that we can ever get our act together and live with each other and nature in complete harmony and peace?

Although I don't see much hope for the survival of our superficial, neurotic, self-centred and dysfunctional civilisation, I certainly feel that a world full of love, harmony and peace is a distinct possibility. I am convinced that humanity really does have the potential to let go of all conflict and misery, and thus live in total inner and outer freedom. If you look at the sorry state that the world is in at the moment, such a scenario might seem utterly utopian and perhaps even laughable to some people, but is it really so far-fetched to suggest that we can have unconditional love in our hearts, harmony in all our relationships and peace on Earth?

When looking at the world with all its conflicts, wars, poverty, misery and destruction of nature, it is very easy to come to the conclusion that something is quite obviously terribly wrong. It doesn't take much intelligence to see that humanity is in a very troublesome spot indeed, almost beyond hope, but we would do well to remember that night is at its darkest just before dawn starts to break.

Many bright and intelligent people down through the centuries have looked at man's incessant wars and conflicts, the cruelty, malice and exploitation that is going on, and said that it is like this because of how society is organised. So they have tried to change society, and thus create a better world, but that has all been rather futile. History has shown us time and time again that even if you do manage to change society to some extent, the change is only ever on the surface. Exploitation, corruption, abuse and other vices still carry on. This is because the real root of the problem is not so much how society is organised. It goes much deeper than that; right to the very core of the human psyche.

It may be possible to organise society in such a way that at least it looks like everybody more or less has equal rights and lives a fairly decent and prosperous life. This has been tried in various ways, such as experiments with communism and various other ideological models, but regardless of what system has been tried out, a new power elite has always emerged and subjugated the majority of people in some way or other. The political solution doesn't really work in other words, because it is only a treatment of symptoms, and doesn't go to the root cause of the problem. Fighting for a better and more just world and introducing legislation to combat injustice and crime may all be well and good, but it can't really provide any lasting solutions. For example, it is good to have laws against corruption and try to fight it that way, but corruption will only be a thing of the past once the human mind is completely free from greed.

How can you ever hope to change the world for the better if you haven't first changed yourself? How can we ever hope to bring about harmony in the world if we're still full of inner conflict? Isn't it obvious that for anything to change in the world in a fundamental way, what really has to change is the way we function and how we relate to one another? Peace on Earth will only become a reality if there is peace within each and every one of us.

As long as we continue to be power-hungry, violent, angry, jealous, possessive, vindictive, and all the rest of it, the world is going to remain the same. It is only when we live from a state of love, harmony and peace that these qualities will manifest themselves outwardly. When realising this, some people try to change themselves through whatever means they feel are useful. They may take up meditation and other spiritual or religious disciplines, or various forms of therapy and self-development practices, or maybe they start reading self-help books and suchlike in the hope of making positive changes to themselves. That's all fine and dandy, and even helpful in some ways, but it doesn't touch the fundamental core of the problem, because all such activities still operate within the narrow framework of the ego wanting or trying to improve or to achieve something for itself. It is absolutely crucial to understand that the me or ego, which is what most people seem to think they are, is essentially nothing more than a functional entity. It might seem to exist as seen from a practical point of view, but it is not something that is actually real, so anything gained through its activities will ultimately come to nothing.

So what exactly is the root cause of the many problems facing humanity? It is quite simply that we have individually and collectively developed a sense of identity that is utterly false. We have been conditioned and brainwashed right from the beginning into believing that we are all separate entities, living in a material world that exists as the fundamental bedrock of reality, independent of consciousness itself. We take it for granted that we are a limited person residing inside a human body. Everybody else and the world itself are distinctive from the person that we identify with, and so life is an endless struggle in which only the fittest, cleverest, craftiest, smartest and most cunning will survive, prosper and win. This is the root of all the world's conflicts, and as long as this sense of mistaken identity is still alive within us, all our problems, wars, conflicts, strife, struggle and misery will continue to manifest themselves in one way or another.

The person, the me, the ego, is really nothing more than a

kind of entity that has a role to play purely on a practical level, but it doesn't refer to anything that is ultimately real. We are nothing rather than something, nobody rather than somebody. There is only ever the one universal consciousness expressing itself as the many. All the myriad forms of life in the universe, and in all non-physical realms as well, ethereal, astral or whatever they might be, are only temporary expressions of that which is beyond them all.

Once we see this, and realise our true nature to be that of unlimited, universal consciousness, the natural, effortless response is one of love, or we could say that love is the fragrance of spiritual realisation, of knowing who you are. Love is truly the only thing that can create a new Earth of peace and harmony. Love in this sense is not so much a feeling; it is not even a state of mind; it is quite simply the essence of what we are. Once this natural, effortless and unconditional love shines forth, the darkness of fear, hate, violence and selfishness disappears like the darkness of the night evaporates at sunrise.

Everything that is happening to us on our journey through life is in the hands of life itself, and to have any preconceived ideas about how it should all be working out is of no use. Nobody is actually doing anything, it's all just happening. It's life expressing itself in whatever way it does. When you don't insist on taking ownership of anything, you may also realise that only life itself is running the show, and that all ideas of I, me, my and mine are at best only tools on a practical level. They don't really mean anything and conflicts arise only when we build a makeshift entity, an ego, and believe that that's what we are. That's when things get complicated and difficult. That's not to say that we won't pass through difficult experiences and emotions occasionally, because that's just part of how life works, but we won't be bogged down by any of it if we let life and love flow without the ego getting in the way.

Life is full of paradoxes and the greatest one is that while we are all mortal, we are also the immortal; that which never was born and never can die. We are the eternal, which means that death should hold no terror for us. Some time ago I was talking with somebody about the possibility of life after death and was asked if I ever felt worried or fearful about what might happen when I die. I responded: "No, of course not. Why should I be afraid? I have friends in high places!" Joking aside, what is there really to be afraid of? Death could only ever be scary or something we should try to avoid at all costs if we believe we are a separate entity that has an independent existence, and that our ultimate salvation or damnation is decided by some imaginary God. I can certainly see how that could be a very scary prospect indeed: What if the old dude is in a foul mood when it's your time to be judged? That would be seriously unfortunate, and doesn't really bear thinking about. Well, I have good news for you, because as it happens, there is no God in that sense. That kind of God was created by man in his own image, and it is all just religious claptrap; a monumental lie and disastrous misunderstanding of what God truly is.

However, there is certainly death, and there's no point pretending otherwise. But that's fine, because death is our eternal companion, our most loyal friend and will never let us down. Now, there's a soothing and comforting thought for you! Yet in spite of the absolute certainty of death being utterly dependable, in truth there is actually no death. There is only ever life in all its magnificent, unfathomable, multidimensional glory and splendour. While it's true that we are all mortal on the level of form, it's equally true that in essence we are eternal, limitless, immortal, universal consciousness. As long as we fully embody and live our lives from that realisation, all will be well.

What you think of as your life is the ultimate expression of creativity, and can be thought of as a giant work of art effortlessly painted on a very large, multidimensional canvas. Most of us usually think of life as a linear process running from past, through the present and into the future, starting at birth and ending at death, but it doesn't really work like that. We experience life through the medium of psychological time only because the human mind has been conditioned throughout thousands of years to perceive it like that. Life as we know it is a manifestation in form of universal consciousness and transcends all our limited and limiting ideas of time and space.

I'll try to give you a better feel for what I mean by this by giving you an idea of how I see what we can think of as "my life". The entire story of my life is one singular process of wholeness where everything is being created simultaneously in this eternal moment, the only moment there ever is. My birth, childhood, adolescence, adulthood, old age and death are all being created, lived and experienced in this eternal now. How long my life is ultimately going to be in terms of calendar years is of no importance whatsoever. It is only my degree of self-knowledge and ability to manifest and express unconditional love that can ever make any real difference.

A different way of looking at this is to use the metaphor of a soap bubble or a balloon. Think of an individual life form like a soap bubble or a balloon. A small bubble symbolises a short life span, and a bigger bubble would indicate a longer life span. If you enlarge the soap bubble or blow the balloon bigger, you will extend the life span, but what happens to the events of that lifetime if you do that? The events for that life will be more or less the same, only more spread out, maybe with less apparent intensity to them. But you don't really have to extend your life span beyond what's natural for your particular manifestation in this world, because it's not a question of quantity, but of quality. It is a question of creating, manifesting and sharing unconditional love. That is what ultimately determines whether any particular expression of universal consciousness is a worthwhile adventure or not.

This is also what determines the ultimate fate of humanity

itself. At the present time it would appear that humanity is in a truly shocking and utterly hopeless state. We are behaving like a bunch of irresponsible teenagers driving at high speed in a shiny, luxurious car straight towards the edge of a very high cliff, oblivious to the fact that our recklessness and ignorance will soon send us straight over the edge and down into the abyss below. That kind of scenario can only end in an almighty, spectacular crash and burn. We might have a vague, uneasy sense that something like this is what is happening, but we are so caught up in our modern affluent lifestyle, so mesmerised by all our gadgets, gizmos and high-tech tomfoolery that we just refuse to see where we are actually heading.

We might think that we are highly developed and sophisticated, but aren't all our conflicts, wars, misery and suffering clear evidence that we are still very primitive and immature in so many ways? Why do we continue to treat each other and Mother Earth the way we do? Why do we insist on acting like such complete and utter morons? The answer is simple; we have built a fake identity, forever chasing after fulfilment on the level of form. We all too often fail to realise the simple truth that fulfilment can never be found on any level of form, regardless of whether that form is material, astral, spiritual or anything else. We are so convinced that we are a separate identity, an ego, a me versus you, that it would never even occur to most of us that this is exactly where the source of the world's problems ultimately is to be found.

Irrespective of all our well-meaning efforts to create peace and justice in the world, as long as a fake identity built around false and superficial values runs the show, nothing is ever going to change. We can continue to deceive ourselves for as long as we want, stupidly doling out peace prizes and similar ridiculous awards to a seemingly never-ending supply of despicable warmongers and certified twerps, but in effect we are just creating more havoc, war and conflict, and destroying each other, nature and the beautiful Earth in the process.

What is so sorely missing in our selfish, shallow and technology-obsessed world is the realisation that at heart we are all one. We are one universal consciousness expressing and exploring itself through an infinite number of forms and appearances. When we realise the true nature of who we are and what life is, an authentic spiritual life of mindfulness and compassion effortlessly manifests through us. It is the full expression of unconditional love that will ultimately transform this world for the better and make humanity reach its highest and most noble potential. And then we may also have the pleasure of enjoying the effortless ease of being conscious co-creators in the ever-unfolding mystery of life.

We seem to have forgotten how to love unconditionally, without expecting or wanting anything in return. This love isn't something that comes and goes; it is ever present, knows only giving, and is the only love that is ultimately real. It exists for its own sake and has no other reason for being and manifesting than celebrating and expressing itself in all its creative glory. When we surrender and let go of all control, we may finally love with total abandon. When we open up to the power of love, we also learn to fully enjoy and appreciate this exhilarating ride we think of as life. When we let love guide our lives, spontaneous gratitude for the gifts that life is giving us naturally follows, and thus the power of love does become the leading light in our lives. You could say that this is when we have truly arrived, even though there isn't really anyone to arrive anywhere, or anything to achieve either for that matter. There is just the joyous expression of life itself, and if we allow it all to unfold naturally and in its own inimitable way, our lives can be the most wonderful manifestation of unconditional love, immense beauty, effortless creativity and unbridled passion.

When we realise that all is one and that there is no me or you actually doing anything, that we are all expressions of the same universal consciousness, the same divine being, then and only then will we know peace on Earth. That is when the glory of love will shine forth in all its power, beauty and wonder. That is when we will finally have returned to the Garden, to Paradise on Earth.

The Enchanted Garden

Softly unfolding, flowers laughing
The joy of this spontaneous creative outburst
Exploding gracefully through all our senses
Yielding to everything yet conquering all
Watching shapes and colours spring to life
Finding you here is the greatest delight
So unexpected, a sense of destiny being fulfilled

A lovely new twist to the age-old story
The journey continues further on
Delving ever deeper into the miracle of life
Beyond the beauty of this enchanted garden
Perfect brilliant stillness forever prevails

Thank you for reading this book. I hope you enjoyed it, and if you would like to read more, you may also want to explore my website at https://pathikstrand.com. If you have any comments or questions about what you have read, you are most welcome to get in touch using the contact form on the website. Please feel free to add your review of the book on your favourite online websites as well.

Pathik Strand

O-BOOKS
SPIRITUALITY

O is a symbol of the world, of oneness and unity; this eye represents knowledge and insight. We publish titles on general spirituality and living a spiritual life. We aim to inform and help you on your own journey in this life.
If you have enjoyed this book, why not tell other readers by posting a review on your preferred book site?

Recent bestsellers from O-Books are:

Heart of Tantric Sex
Diana Richardson
Revealing Eastern secrets of deep love and intimacy to Western couples.
Paperback: 978-1-90381-637-0 ebook: 978-1-84694-637-0

Crystal Prescriptions
The A-Z guide to over 1,200 symptoms and their healing crystals
Judy Hall
The first in the popular series of six books, this handy little guide is packed as tight as a pill-bottle with crystal remedies for ailments.
Paperback: 978-1-90504-740-6 ebook: 978-1-84694-629-5

The Holy Spirit's Interpretation of the New Testament
A Course in Understanding and Acceptance
Regina Dawn Akers
Following on from the strength of *A Course In Miracles*, NTI
teaches us how to experience the love and oneness of God.
Paperback: 978-1-84694-085-9 ebook: 978-1-78099-083-5

The Message of A Course In Miracles
A translation of the Text in plain language
Elizabeth A. Cronkhite
A translation of *A Course in Miracles* into plain, everyday
language for anyone seeking inner peace. The companion
volume, *Practicing A Course In Miracles*, offers practical lessons
and mentoring.
Paperback: 978-1-84694-319-5 ebook: 978-1-84694-642-4

Your Simple Path
Find Happiness in every step
Ian Tucker
A guide to helping us reconnect with what is really important in
our lives.
Paperback: 978-1-78279-349-6 ebook: 978-1-78279-348-9

365 Days of Wisdom
Daily Messages To Inspire You Through The Year
Dadi Janki
Daily messages which cool the mind, warm the heart and guide
you along your journey.
Paperback: 978-1-84694-863-3 ebook: 978-1-84694-864-0

Body of Wisdom
Women's Spiritual Power and How it Serves
Hilary Hart
Bringing together the dreams and experiences of women across
the world with today's most visionary spiritual teachers.
Paperback: 978-1-78099-696-7 ebook: 978-1-78099-695-0

Dying to Be Free
From Enforced Secrecy to Near Death to True Transformation
Hannah Robinson
After an unexpected accident and near-death experience, Hannah
Robinson found herself radically transforming her life, while a
remarkable new insight altered her relationship with her father, a
practising Catholic priest.
Paperback: 978-1-78535-254-6 ebook: 978-1-78535-255-3

The Ecology of the Soul
A Manual of Peace, Power and Personal Growth for Real People
in the Real World
Aidan Walker
Balance your own inner Ecology of the Soul to regain your
natural state of peace, power and wellbeing.
Paperback: 978-1-78279-850-7 ebook: 978-1-78279-849-1

Not I, Not other than I
The Life and Teachings of Russel Williams
Steve Taylor, Russel Williams
The miraculous life and inspiring teachings of one of the World's
greatest living Sages.
Paperback: 978-1-78279-729-6 ebook: 978-1-78279-728-9

On the Other Side of Love
A woman's unconventional journey towards wisdom
Muriel Maufroy
When life has lost all meaning, what do you do?
Paperback: 978-1-78535-281-2 ebook: 978-1-78535-282-9

Practicing A Course In Miracles
A translation of the Workbook in plain language, with
mentor's notes
Elizabeth A. Cronkhite
The practical second and third volumes of The Plain-Language
A Course In Miracles.
Paperback: 978-1-84694-403-1 ebook: 978-1-78099-072-9

Quantum Bliss
The Quantum Mechanics of Happiness, Abundance, and Health
George S. Mentz
Quantum Bliss is the breakthrough summary of success and
spirituality secrets that customers have been waiting for.
Paperback: 978-1-78535-203-4 ebook: 978-1-78535-204-1

Readers of ebooks can buy or view any of these bestsellers by
clicking on the live link in the title. Most titles are published
in paperback and as an ebook. Paperbacks are available in
traditional bookshops. Both print and ebook formats are
available online.
Find more titles and sign up to our readers' newsletter at
http://www.johnhuntpublishing.com/mind-body-spirit
Follow us on Facebook at https://www.facebook.com/OBooks/
and Twitter at https://twitter.com/obooks